MW00850928

Travels with Ferdinand and Friends:
A Centennial Journey Through Austria-Hungary
WINNER OF THE PANTHER CREEK
NONFICTION BOOK AWARD

Hidden River Arts offers the Panther Creek Nonfiction Book Award yearly for an unpublished book length work of nonfiction. The award provides $1,000 and publication by Hidden River Press.

Hidden River Arts is an interdisciplinary arts organization dedicated to supporting and celebrating the unserved artists among us, particularly those outside the artistic and academic mainstream.

Travels with Ferdinand and Friends

A Centennial Journey Through Austria-Hungary

Mark Eliot Nuckols

HIDDEN RIVER PRESS
An imprint of Hidden River Publishing
Philadelphia, Pennsylvania

Cover, interior design and typography by : Jana Rade

Library of Congress Control Number 2021952697
ISBN 978-0-9994915-9-1

HIDDEN RIVER PRESS
An imprint of Hidden River Publishing
Philadelphia, Pennsylvania

DEDICATION

*In memory of my father, Melvin G. Nuckols (1929-2022),
who awoke my desire to see the world with his stories of
service in the U.S. Army in the Philippines and Germany*

PROLOGUE

The year 2014 may already seem an age of innocence by comparison with the tumultuous early 2020s. My recollections may give the impression of escapism. But Travels with Ferdinand and Friends also centers on 1914, and, while pining for pre-World War I Europe, it deals with the geo-political events that led to the horrors of the trenches and poison gas, shattering illusions about unmitigated progress. Just as importantly, my story balances history with the human experience of the Here and Now: the meals and the music; conversations with strangers and old friends; the energy and excitement, the fatigue and frustration that come with exploring other lands. It reminds us to live in the moment, while observing reminders of the past.

Those culinary and other sensations of travel abroad are harder to come by now, as I write these lines in 2022, over two years since the outbreak of COVID. When not fatal, the virus has still caused some victims to lose taste and smell. As a musician, I've faced restrictions on singing in public. And of course, the pandemic has made international travel a dicey business. Yet it's also brought about solidarity at many levels. Who can forget the videos of people singing to each other from their balconies, the "One World: Together at Home" online concert with Paul McCartney and other leading musicians, or Andrea Bocelli's performance from the cathedral in Milan, capital of the hard-hit Lombardy region?

We've also witnessed the George Floyd protests, and the removal of statues of Robert E. Lee from both Charlottesville—where I went to college—and Richmond, capital of my home state. And while crowds toppled Lenin statues all over East-Central Europe in the 1990s, no one seems in a hurry to remove monuments to the Austrian Habsburgs – although there are plenty of people who obsess over that dynasty's oppression of other nations, which it did at times, though this is often exaggerated in nationalist rhetoric. Interethnic conflict and inequalities in European history are important themes of this book, as are debates over historical memory. Perhaps the displays I observed on my trip, those commemorating the continent's slide into conflict in 1914, can serve as food for thought about preserving the past – with sensitivity as well as accuracy.

Before January 2021, most Americans, as well as outside observers of U.S. politics, could scarcely have imagined a mob storming the U.S. Capitol, disrupting the counting of Electoral College votes for president, as submitted by the states, usually a serene and stately process of confirming the results. Stefan Zweig, the Jewish-Austrian writer whose memoir *The World of Yesterday* plays a large role in the present book, had believed it impossible that Germany would violate Belgium's sovereignty by marching through that country to attack France. I had watched the opening and closing ceremonies to the 2014 Winter Olympics from Sochi with a lump in my throat at the display of Russian contributions to the arts. But my feelings were mixed. I've always felt an affinity to the creative geniuses of that country while distrusting its officialdom. And I knew that, all too typically for any modern Olympic Games, there was plenty of corruption and environmental degradation involved in the construction of the facilities. Finally, I watched a month later as Putin sent his little green men into Crimea. Political stability is not to be taken for granted, nor is the much-vaunted "inviolability of borders." That Crimean Crisis formed part of the backdrop to my European trip in the summer of that year. In the years since, I've had the eerie feeling a full-scale occupation of Ukraine might be in store, yet always entertained the hope that diplomacy would prevail. My optimism was shattered by Putin's invasion of February 2022.

But as I suggested, *Travels with Ferdinand and Friends* is primarily about culture. It offers my encounters with Europeans, including Italians, Austrians, Hungarians, and Slavs of several stripes, as they recalled the tragedy of World War I a century after its outbreak. In these pages you will also find a continent of nearly unimpeded travel, of lax border crossings, thanks to the expansion of the European Union – which is, in some ways, a recreation of the old Holy Roman Empire, founded by Charlemagne in the year 800, and its successor state, the Habsburg empire in Central Europe in the nineteenth and early twentieth centuries.

Thanks to the COVID pandemic that began in 2020, the restrictions it has brought, large refugee influxes coupled with anti-immigrant backlash, and another previously-thought-impossible event, Brexit, travel isn't so simple these days. But while we're waiting for things to return to "normal"—whatever that means—let's enjoy some time on the road, in our minds and on these pages.

By "in our minds," I'm suggesting pleasant imaginings, and

also the fact that a recounting of events like this is a mental reconstruction. I have allowed myself some—but not much—license to embellish, change names, add juiciness to conversations, insert a little scene from another trip, and make slight changes in chronology. But these alterations are minimal.

So, without further ado, let the journey begin!

1

Prague: Hunter and Hunted

I n the restaurant of Konopischt, the former castle of Franz Ferdinand near Prague, small framed black-and-whites of the archduke hang on the creamy stucco walls. In one, he and his uncle, Emperor Franz Joseph, wear white officer's tunics and dark ostrich-feather caps. In a family portrait, he stands in a corner next to a stove in the same uniform, hat in hand, revealing a flat-top. The others sit, boys in black suits with bowties, daughter in white dress with long dark hair draped over a shoulder. Wife

Sophie, tight-waisted dress laced to the neck, copious hair pinned into a bun, gazes adoringly at the children.

The most striking photo shows Ferdinand, family, and guests gathered over a freshly killed ten-point buck. They've all donned traditional gray Austrian hunting outfits for the occasion, except for a couple of bearded servants in darker, slightly rumpled attire, nonetheless wearing ties. The archduke, rifle slung over a shoulder, stares back at me. His pupils seem mere pinpoints, centers of a geometrical design, like an Orthodox icon. The twin curves of his handlebar moustache underscore eye sockets deep and shadowy beneath the brim of a Homburg. An early twentieth-century emoji, but a confusing one. Does it express surprise? Pride over his trophy? Ennui? Sadness at the deer's death? His irises are inscrutable as opals.

A waiter bangs open the swinging doors from the kitchen, rousing me from my reverie. The sizzle and greasy odor of frying veal cutlets drifts into the dining room.

"They should have venison on the menu," I joke to my erstwhile travel companions.

"Or wild boar," says Raj. The wiry Indian-Australian, in polo shirt and khaki shorts, has lively, youthful black eyes, quite unlike those of the Habsburg heir apparent. "This guy was a hunting fanatic."

The server sets our Pilsners—originals, from the Bohemian town of Plzeň—on cardboard coasters. We three guests clink mugs and quaff.

"We've been in Prague for a week-long conference," says Tom, a sandy-haired fortyish Anglo-Australian. "Seen the basic sights. Charles Bridge, the castle, Old Town Square. Nice to get away from the crowds and relax. What brings you here?"

"Well, I've spent seven years in this part of the world. I have friends in Prague. Some in Slovakia, too."

"Visiting any new places?"

"Yes, the Balkans. To Sarajevo for the hundredth anniversary of the assassination."

"Ah," says Raj. "Taking the long way round. But I guess this is a logical starting point. Why all the interest?"

"I learned about the shooting in high school, how it started World War I." I shake my head. "Whole empires unraveled: Austria-Hungary, Ottoman Turkey. Redrew the map of Europe – and a lot of the Middle East."

We sip the frothy, hoppy brews, and lean back in our chairs. I'm grateful for company, since I'm travelling alone. But I'm hesitant to share my nostalgia for a defunct monarchy. Not that I'm crazy about its authoritarianism, but many of the regimes that followed were worse. And it certainly produced some great composers: Haydn, Mozart, two Strausses, operettas in the late nineteenth and early twentieth centuries, and even some very experimental music like Schönberg. It also gave us Freud. Many of his observations were penetrating; others, merely speculative – but still fascinating. He's not taught that much in psychology departments anymore, but literary critics can't seem to resist Freudian interpretation. Likely no one has more greatly influenced how we think about how we think – or caused us to question what our true motives are.

Speaking of which, my *conscious* objective on this long pilgrimage is to stay within the former Austria-Hungary while covering several of its successor states, including Bosnia and Herzegovina, Croatia, Slovenia, and Italy. Alps, Danube, Adriatic Coast. To visit parts of the empire I've not seen before, to become re-acquainted with others and see how they've changed in the years since I lived here. To observe how they commemorate this tragic centenary. To reconnect with old friends – and make new ones. Where my unconscious desires and serendipity lead me is another question.

I met Raj and Tom on a double-decker train. We viewed surrounding hills and fields for the forty-five minute ride through Prague's outskirts, where terraced vineyards alternated with forests and rows of cottages with fenced-in garden plots, the second home people could own under socialism without fear of the bourgeois label.

Now we drink in silence for a few moments. Tom remarks, "But the Czechs are none too nostalgic about the Habsburgs."

"No wonder. The Austrians dominated them for three centuries. They don't recall the Russians fondly, either. Especially after the invasion of sixty-eight."

We sip more beer, wipe foam from our lips.

"I'm reading Stefan Zweig's *The World of Yesterday*," I say to keep the conversation going. "His memoir about how Europe unraveled in World War I. And later."

"Wait a minute," says Raj. "Wasn't he the inspiration for *Grand Budapest Hotel*?"

"Wes Anderson's film. I saw it in March when it first came out." I chuckle. "And again on the flight over. Some of the images come straight from the Czech Republic. The statue of a stag atop a precipice, the salmon hotel."

Tom frowns. "So what's the connection between the film and this writer?"

"Zweig was a Jewish Austrian who ended up a stateless exile after the Anschluss. Kinda like the concierge Ralph Fiennes played.

The world around him became unrecognizable."

Our waiter saunters in with Tom and Raj's Wiener Schnitzel, hammered so thin and wide it hangs over the plates. I have beef goulash. It's not the Hungarian soup, but a thick variation served on a plate with *knedlíky*, like German *Knödel*, porous bread dumplings for sopping the almost-black gravy.

It strikes me how the book and the movie both pine for a lost culture. In the preface to *The World of Yesterday*, the author laments:

"I was born in 1881 in a great and mighty empire, in the monarchy of the Habsburgs. But do not look for it on the map; it has been swept away without a trace. I grew up in Vienna, the two-thousand-year-old super-national metropolis, and was forced to leave it like a criminal before it was degraded to a German provincial city."

The film's opening echoes Zweig's words with the silent white titles *The former Republic of Zubrowka, once the seat of an Empire.*

Anderson places his fictional land somewhere "on the eastern boundaries of Europe." The soundtrack's Alpine yodeling, Hungarian hammer dulcimer, and balalaikas evoke the ethnic diversity of the old Habsburg Monarchy – though Russian instruments would have been out of place there. Anderson also conflates both world wars, adding touches of absurdity: soldiers in long gray Central Powers overcoats crunch about in the snow; officers of the Z, in black SS-like uniforms, stomp into the flamboyant pink Deco Grand Budapest lobby and set up headquarters there, hanging their black banners with double Z's reminiscent of the Nazi SS symbol.

After lunch my new comrades and I go outside, since our

2:15 tour starts from the other side of the complex. It'll be in Russian—it's that or wait another hour—but the museum provides hand-held English audio guides. We circle the creamy-white castle, with terracotta tiles on its pointy round main tower, and pause at a terrace. It overlooks the hilly forest, dense with conifers, linden trees, and poplars, where Franz Ferdinand once avidly pursued game.

Raj looks up at a bronze statue of a Greco-Roman figure, spear in hand, leaning back to restrain two dogs on leashes. "Sooo, continuing that hunting theme..."

Tom, shielding his eyes from the sun, nods.

At the entrance we join a Russian family of four, who could be tourists or some of the tens of thousands of their nationality who've settled in the Czech Republic in recent years.

Our guide soon ushers us up a creaking wooden staircase and along a corridor teeming with stuffed deer, bears, bison, gazelles, and antlers galore. A brass plaque labels a mounted pheasant as Ferdinand's seventy-five-thousandth kill.

Tom gasps, eyes bulging.

Raj shakes his head and chuckles. "My guidebook says he bagged nearly three hundred thousand animals."

"Before being gunned down himself," Tom points out.

"My God!" I gasp. "That's excessive even by the standards of his time. At least far fewer species faced extinction back then."

"And there were no PETA protests," Raj quips. The three of us chortle a bit guiltily. Our guide, now twenty feet ahead of us, apparently eager to move on, winces at the boisterousness. With a little clearing of throats, we calm down and follow her into the first room.

Tom and Raj hold the black audio devices, like mobile phones from the 1980s, to their ears. As a linguist, I feel compelled to listen to the guide. Gray-haired with a well-proportioned face, she speaks Russian slowly enough I can catch nearly every word. She points at renaissance paintings and Empire furnishings as she describes them, which helps. My main distraction is her accent, a tendency to stress the first syllable of every word, very alien to Russian, even if Czech is a Slavic cousin. The initial stress in Czech likely resulted from a thousand years of Germanic influence and domination. While I can pick out her flaws, I must admit her Russian vocabulary is far better than mine. Then again, she may have just memorized this spiel. Probably been giving it for twenty-five years, since the days when Russian was a compulsory school subject.

As we view parlors and bedrooms with paintings of various periods and styles, I muse on the privileges of Ferdinand's peers a century ago. Servants did menial duties like beating the bushes to scare up the quail and, after the hunt, plucking feathers, skinning, dressing, and cooking the meat. The archduke also had a staffer to catalog his taxidermy items.

Not to mention his other belongings. After the main tour, we take a self-guided walk around the St. George Hall, a cool downstairs room with a vaulted white ceiling, and red and green marble floor tiles. It's loaded with paintings and carvings of the saint killing the fabled dragon in several centuries of renderings.

Back out in the sun, Tom says, "I'm not sure whether to call this guy a connoisseur or a hoarder. We haven't even seen his collection of medieval armor. Supposed to be the third largest in Europe."

After another chuckle, Raj looks at his watch. "We'd better be heading back. There's a conference dinner at six."

"Have a safe trip back to Australia," I say as we shake hands.

"And you have a nice journey around Franz Ferdinand's old

Austria," says Tom. They soon disappear down a winding path lined with tall, unclipped shrubbery.

Left alone, I turn back to the castle once more. Although I'm beginning to see the archduke's potential for cupidity and violence, an exhibit in another wing promises to reveal his tender side. Called "Together in Life and Death," it reflects on his marriage to Sophie Chotek.

Among items from the archduke's childhood in the glass cases is a Czech textbook. However boorish he may have been, he grew to speak the language fluently, along with his native German. He spent much of his adult life in and around Prague, where, by some accounts, he met his future wife at an aristocratic party, instantly taken with her. Although a countess, Sophie lacked the "dynastic rank" of a ruling family. Ferdinand's choice ignited a major row with his uncle, Franz Joseph. The successor to the imperial throne marrying so far beneath his estate! After months of agonizing, they reached a compromise: Ferdinand could succeed as emperor *and* wed Sophie, but he had to renounce their children's claim to the throne.

I pause at another vitrine, displaying photos of the couple and a yellowed copy of the agreement on the morganatic marriage. The House of Habsburg took every opportunity to humiliate her, forbidding her to appear at FF's side during ceremonies of state. Franz Joseph refused to attend the wedding, and discouraged archdukes and archduchesses from doing so, as well. But Franz Ferdinand, authoritarian and capricious as he seems to have been, had enough of a soft spot to break with tradition and marry for love.

In another display case hang photos from German Kaiser Wilhelm II's visit to Konopischt in early June 1914, and faded documents on Ferdinand's upcoming trip to Bosnia to inspect maneuvers. A map of the parade route through the streets of Sarajevo was published well in advance, giving the assassins ample time to plan the attack, a security lapse unimaginable in our day. No wonder some people still bounce around conspiracy theories about a setup.

Letters, bulletins and newspapers show the response to the killings back in Bohemia. Some express concern for the orphans' welfare. A final glass case displays a picture of the monument to the victims which was erected in Sarajevo near the spot – but torn down after World War I, when Bosnia became part of the new Yugoslavia, the "Land of the South Slavs."

Back outside in the rose garden I recognize another of the archduke's obsessions. He'd selected and ordered hundreds of varieties of cuttings and root stock, and planted and grafted them himself – presumably with some help from the domestics. I picture him with sleeves rolled up, spade in hand, though protocol probably forbade photos of him in such a casual state. That June of a hundred years ago the family had opened the grounds to visitors – everyone from Kaiser Wilhelm to local peasants and workers had flocked to see the flowers.

It's about seventy-five Fahrenheit now, with only a few clouds in sight. For a moment, the sunshine makes the bloody tragedy of a century ago feel distant. Then I recall that the fateful June of 1914 had offered the best weather anyone could remember. A Europe-wide conflagration, let alone a world war, had been unimaginable to generations accustomed to steady nineteenth-century progress. When the Berlin Wall came down in 1989, I'd almost believed it was the "end of history." Only two years later I observed firsthand the events that led to the relatively amicable split of Czechoslovakia – and saw sorrow in the eyes of Slovak friends who were suddenly and bitterly arguing over politics with Czech spouses. From there I followed on TV the outbreak of fratricide in the rapidly disintegrating Yugoslavia. Now, in 2014, there's fighting between Russians and Ukrainians in Donbass, something else I'd never anticipated.

I stroll among the roses – surely there were more in FF's day. And what about other vegetation? The property's Czech name, *Konopiště*, derives from the Slavic for cannabis: the "hemp field." I've never found any mention of whether the archduke cultivated it, like George Washington at Mount Vernon, presumably to make rope and twine, or whether it just grew wild. But for all the supposed severity of the old monarchy, it never got seriously into the business of regulating such substances. As in most Western countries around 1900, one could buy cocaine prescription-free in pharmacies. Freud openly experimented on himself with the stimulant, initially writing of it as a miracle drug, but it nearly ruined his health and career.

As male peacocks fan their iridescent feathers and shimmy them with a dry-sounding rattle, a Roma mother pushes a baby carriage along the fine gravel. Two daughters skip around, sandals crunching. Ah, the "Gypsy" minority, long pushed around in an empire which never had a majority. Perhaps I, the white male from Virginia, am over-romanticizing an association of this ethnicity with freedom, but I'm looking forward to meeting Roma musicians on my trip – and hearing their music.

* * *

Back in Prague, I call Peter, a violinist I got to know when I would hang out in a hotel restaurant to listen to his ensemble in the late nineties. It was a typical Gypsy band, with Peter leading, his brother on *cimbal* (hammer dulcimer), and a standup bass and viola.

That was in Košice, East Slovakia, the country's second largest city at about a quarter million. His brother and the bass player passed away a decade ago; so now, at around fifty, my age, Peter has moved his entire family here from Slovakia so they can be with his son, who's recently begun conservatory studies for violin. Peter is the graduate of a less prominent conservatory, so this is a big step up for his family.

Unlike the stereotype of Roma as ragged street musicians with battered guitars, who drink up their tips as fast as they can make them, Peter rarely imbibes and patiently saves his money for top-quality instruments, and good clothes. He always shows up to work in jacket and tie, with neatly pressed slacks and shirt. When I last visited him three years ago, he and other Roma were watching Budapest Gypsy groups on his widescreen. Entertainment, professional development, and a strong cultural connection with the land just to their south – they all spoke Hungarian, as well as Slovak and Romani. Atop the baby grand in Peter's living room were two adult-sized violins and one for a child – the fiddle his son had first learned on. Many people say Roma have a genetic disposition for music. I've wondered about it, having heard the flawless intonation of even untrained singers, but I suspect it has more to do with starting very young. Clearly there's a strong element of musical upbringing in this family.

"Mark, sorry you missed me," Peter tells me on the phone. "I'm back in Slovakia, playing at the National Theater. In *The Czardas Princess*. You saw me in it the last time you were in Europe, right?"

It's the operetta by Emmerich Kálmán. Composed in autumn 1914, as Austria-Hungary was going to war. A young nobleman and a cabaret singer, in love, struggle to get his mother's approval to marry, a lot like Franz Ferdinand and Sophie Chotek. The nobleman's mother turns out to have been a singer herself before marrying into higher status.

"When are you going to be back in Prague?" I ask.

"Friday."

"Damn, I'll be on my way to Slovakia then."

"And after that?"

"To Hungary, then Sarajevo. But I'm flying back home from Prague. In five weeks. Guess I'll have to see you then."

I reminisce on *The Czardas Princess*, with its mingling of classes and cultures. Kálmán, of Jewish-Hungarian birth, fused those influences with Viennese waltz. Add in some Slavic and Romani elements and you've got the melting pot of the early twentieth-century capital. Hitler wrote in *Mein Kampf* of his revulsion at the *Rassenmischung*, or "mix of races," that he'd found upon moving to Vienna in his youth. Just the kind of thing I'm here to delight in!

2

Goulash Party in "Zubrowka"

My initial plan was to take a week to visit Kraków and L'viv in the old Galician part of the empire. But just before departing the States, I was invited to a goulash party for a Slovak chorus I'd belonged to in the nineties. We sang everything from Händel and Bruckner to four-part arrangements of folk tunes, performed at commemorative events and historic sites. Our unofficial program always involved dancing, laughing, drinking and impromptu music.

This weekend should be no different.

My train crosses the Czech-Slovak border with nary a pause, just like it was when I lived there from 1990-92. Then I returned to Virginia for an M.A. program, and when I came back in autumn 1993, Czechoslovakia had split up. Passport control became the norm, even between these two intimate countries. Now, with both nations in the European Union, the border is little more than a formality, as when they were part of the old Empire. In the nineties the trains clunked along uneven rail joints, compartments had burgundy vinyl seat covers. Doors and windows would hang up, then suddenly come unstuck with a bang. These days, thanks largely to EU investments, we glide along smooth tracks, in cars with bright blue cloth seats; a mere tap of a handle opens the hydraulic doors between carriages.

As I stand to stretch, a thirty-year-old conductor in navy slacks and vest with orange-brown trim swaggers down the aisle. "You'll have to get out in Žilina."

"Why? Doesn't this train go all the way to Zvolen?"

"It does. You just have to get in another car."

"You mean another wagon on this train?"

He frowns over a hatchet-blade nose. "It's connected to another locomotive."

"So it's ... another train?"

He sighs and shakes his head. "Same train, Prague to Zvolen."

"Then why do I have to change?"

He throws up his hands. "Because it's a different *súprava*."

Ah, *súprava*, the arrangement of a given express: locomotive, first- and second-class wagons, dining and baggage cars. So I'll be on the same train only in the sense that it's the same route, but a different set of coaches. Before I can ask more questions, he hastens down the aisle, repeating the announcement to other passengers, much like surly officials in Austria-Hungary – or in Wes Anderson's Zubrowka.

In *Grand Budapest Hotel*, jut-jawed soldiers in bulky gray overcoats sling open the compartment door of Grand Budapest concierge Monsieur Gustav and lobby boy Zero Moustafa, demanding ID. The teenage Middle Eastern war refugee swallows and pulls out a tattered, handwritten slip of paper. Smirks spread on the guards' razor-stubble faces. M. Gustav has the audacity to reason with them, for which he and Zero both get their noses bloodied. But during the fracas an officer happens by, recognizes Gustav, and assures Zero unimpeded travel.

The woolen overcoats remind me of the illustrations to *The Good Soldier Švejk*, Jaroslav Hašek's 1920s satire about the Austro-Hungarian army in World War I. Sadistic officers, invariably German-speakers, kick Czech privates in the butt, or yell at them, baring teeth under push-broom moustaches. Its intractable officials inspired *Catch 22*, and perhaps had something to do with Wes Anderson's minor characters.

Despite all its bureaucracy, Jewish-Austrian novelist Robert Musil wrote wistfully of the land he coined Kakania. The name derives from the German abbreviation K&K for "imperial and royal," referring to the Austrian Empire and the Kingdom of Hungary, the two parts of the Dual Monarchy created by the 1867 Compromise. In his magnum opus *The Man Without Qualities*, Musil finds the magic far from the officialdom of Vienna and Budapest:

Glaciers and sea, karst limestone and Bohemian fields of grain, nights on the Adriatic chirping with restless cicadas, and Slovakian villages where the smoke rose from chimneys as from upturned nostrils while the village cowered between two small hills as if the earth had parted its lips to warm its child between them.

This is the very land I've come to rediscover. It's a land where the people welcomed me, took care of me, when I arrived as a lone Westerner just after the fall of the Communist regime. It's the land where I first learned to sing in another language after falling in love with the folk melodies and harmonies. Now I'm back to sing with old choir friends around an outdoor fire, which will be heating a kettle of stew. I'm here for a goulash party, a get-together common in June, at the end of the school year or concert season in Slovakia.

In Žilina, I have to change trains, lugging my twenty-gallon backpack, laptop bag, and guitar. I call it—uh, her—Emilia. She stays safe in a shiny, heavy-duty black case bought especially for this journey. Anyway, the transfer is but a momentary inconvenience in this present-day Zubrowka.

* * *

I get a good night's rest at the *Čierna pani*, or "Black Lady," a bed-and-breakfast in the provincial mountain town of Martin, the country's historical capital of culture, nestled between the Greater and Lesser Fatras.

The next morning I find Musil's Slovak idyll in the nearby village of Bystrička. I get off the bus and, guitar in one hand, canvas bag full of wine bottles in the other, tromp a half-mile up a gravel lane past A-frames and bungalows of rough-hewn wood. Near the end of a row of fenced-off garden plots fronting little summer homes, I arrive at the white-washed cottage of my buddy and former fellow chorister Fero. He's about fifteen years older than me, sang in the tenor section; I was in bass. A skilled metal worker, he always found ways to connect with everyone in the group, regardless of education, religious or other background. When travelling outside his own country, he was insatiably curious about other people's perspectives. He would put an arm around my shoulder and teasingly call me *Amerika*, as if I were the personification of my country. He respectfully listened to my views while also being frank about his own: America can sell its weapons all over the world, but I'm going to lose my job because we can't sell tanks to Syria.

Twenty choir members, young and old, gather around benches under awnings. Split birch and pine smolder under a twenty-five-gallon stainless stock pot. Mm, the earthy scent of beef and potatoes. I haven't been to a goulash party in two decades. Evergreens rise on the hill to the west, a pasture with sheep slopes gently from there down to the lane, and a brook gurgles and churns just behind the small yard. The blue-gray ridges of the Fatras spread to the east like a bunched-up blanket. That last image reminds me of the tranquil view I enjoyed at breakfast every morning, from the picture window of a school canteen. That was at Gymnázium V.P.-Tótha, on the other side of town, where I first worked here in 1990.

Fero, in graying brown beard and floppy farmer's hat, bounds out of his one-and-a-half-story cabin. "Mark!" He opens his arms wide. After a quick hug, he pours me a shot of home-made plum brandy, *slivovica*. "Comes from the trees right here. I also have cherry"—he points to one side then the other—"and peach."

I double-cheek-kiss with Daniela, a sixty-year-old I last saw when she was forty. Her reddish, neck-length hair is now streaked with gray. A new guest shows up at the gate, and I recognize the aquiline nose of Milan, whose two daughters sang in the choir, though he was not in it himself, back in my day. He shakes a few hands and then gasps, seeing my face.

"*Mark! Ježiš Mária!* What are *you* doing here?"

He tells me he joined the group two years ago and brings me up to date on the lives of his daughters Dana and Gabriela. The younger, Gabriela, had been a student of mine in her senior year of high school. That first December, after I'd been in Martin for only two months, I taught simple English-language Christmas carols to her class, a group of thirty girls and one boy following an arts-oriented curriculum. At the end of the lesson, her classmates encouraged her to stand and sing the Slovak version of "Silent Night." She filled the room with her voice, gliding effortlessly up to the highest notes, treating the phrases with delicate alternations between piano and forte. This Christmas present from her and her class blended artistic talent with personal warmth and was one of many experiences that made me want to stay in Slovakia. Later, I tutored Dana and a friend of hers in Milan's apartment toward the end of my two years in the Martin area, 1990-92. The family took me to their cottage during that second summer. That property had been nationalized—apparently the Communists had considered it excessive wealth, though my Slovak was not good enough in those days to understand all the details—and they'd regained it thanks to new laws on restitution.

Milan holds his chin high. "Gabi's been singing in the opera for twenty years."

I'm not surprised, remembering her piercingly lovely soprano even after so many years.

Soon, the goulash is ready: chunks of beef with strips of onions and green peppers, and, in this Slovak innovation on the Hungarian original, diced *klobasa*. Fero holds out a large shaker of dark-orange powder. "There's already paprika in the goulash, of course, but here's more."

"Any Magyars can have at it!" says a young dark-haired guy. Everyone laughs. Most Slovak cuisine is mildly seasoned, and these mountain Slavs tend to regard the passion for sharp spice of their neighbors from the southern plains as unhealthy. Still, after centuries of Hungarian domination—or should I say despite that painful period?—their table setting looks much like the Magyars', with tricolored shaker sets: black, white, and red for pepper, salt, and paprika.

Fero suddenly blurts, "Hey, Mark. Remember our trip to the choral festival in Hungary? To Ti-sza-vás-vá-ri?" He draws out the syllables of the town's name, making it sound extra-alien, as if to emphasize the Magyars' Asiatic origins. Folks within earshot giggle.

"It was great. So nice you could get along with them."

"They threw a terrific party. What can I say?" He shrugs. "I have no problem with Hungarians," he continues with a scout's-honor expression. Then shakes a finger and adds, "As long as they respect our borders. A lot of them keep maps of Greater Hungary on their walls at home. You know that, don't you?"

I concede his point, not wanting to get into a political argument.

To my relief, he changes the subject – somewhat. "It was on that trip you and Magda got together wasn't it?"

"Yeah, we had a little *techtle-mechtle*," I use the Slovak word, a borrowing from Austrian German, for the 'hanky-panky' with

Magda, which amounted to little more than necking on the bus on the way home. She was a robust and fun-loving musician but ultimately not my type.

"So how come you never married a Slovak girl?" he prods.

"Still haven't found one—of any nationality—I'm sure I'd want to spend my life with." The truth is, I'm starting to wonder if I'm not too set in my ways—or too fiercely independent—at forty-eight. While I'm taking this trip alone (since I don't know anyone else who would do it my way), I'm glad for the company I have now. Some stretches will be lonely without a traveling companion.

Someone pulls out a bagpipe and starts playing. More Slavic than Celtic, it looks like a pillow, tucked under his left arm, with three protrusions: a mouthpiece, a long cylinder that hangs to knee level before bending back up to a flared end like the bell of a skinny saxophone, and a tube with fingerholes which ends in another such bell. There's a wooden goat's head for decoration. As the player bleats a tune, Fero and others warble a simple ditty about lost love.

After a few rowdier folk songs and a subdued patriotic hymn from our old repertoire, I unpack my gut-stringed classical guitar, Emilia, and fire up some Gypsy music. I strum rapidly, Spanish style, the chords to a minor-key "Mr. Postman" I learned from local Roma years ago. I sing the slow, billowing melody, the words of a woman tearing at her hair she's so anxious for a letter from her lover. I hold the last note to build anticipation, then break out in percussive plucking on the lively but wailing refrain. My friends stammer the melody, clueless as to the Romani lyrics, much like *Norteamericanos* singing "Ay, ay, ay, ay" on every line of the Mexican classic "Cielito Lindo." They clap along as the tempo surges, then quiet down as I ease into the second verse.

"I used to play the role of The Gypsy in the theater all the time," says Milan, looking eager to join in. His hair is gray now, but three decades ago, with black curls inherited from his Italian grandfather, he must've really looked the part. We sing a duet of more Romani tunes to the delight of our pals.

A younger guitarist takes over for a while. We toast all around with various drinks, including Fernet Stock, a bitter herb liqueur like Jägermeister, only less dark and syrupy. We play more guitar and bagpipes, pour more shots, and sing a cappella, followed by another round. I manage to stay sober by only taking small sips, thinking: No wonder Hungarians joke about Slovaks being drunk before noon.

I strum and croon "my white wine, from my girlfriend, my red wine, from my other girlfriend" in a Moravian dialect of Czech. All the Slovaks know it and join in, swaying shoulder-to-shoulder.

"Great! Our old American friend comes back and leads us in a Czech song," Fero congratulates me.

For the finale, I whip off "Those Were the Days," a Soviet Gypsy-style tune from the 1920s. The older choristers know the Russian lyrics from years of East-Bloc school lessons; younger ones follow the English. I play it like the postman song, with quick strumming and a plaintive voice on the verses. On the refrains, everyone claps to the building tempo.

A fitting cap to the reunion. After a final toast, a dozen of us amble down to the village's lone bus stop, still catching up on the past twenty-odd years of our lives.

Jana, a retired teacher, points at a two-story manor house which, though not altogether neglected, could use a fresh coat of paint, if not a sandblasting. "Tomáš Garrigue Masaryk's vacation home," she says. "Czechoslovakia's first president."

Masaryk was a Czech philosophy professor, married to an American of French descent. He earned his doctorate in Vienna, where he also served as a parliamentary deputy for a total of nine years in the 1890s and again in the early 1900s. He defended Slavic interests in the Empire. He also angered extreme nationalists by exposing as frauds certain "medieval manuscripts" (forged to give Czechs a millennium-old literary tradition they could pride themselves on), as well as for challenging an accusation of ritual murder against a mentally disabled Jewish man in 1899. Masaryk never argued for the dissolution of Austria-Hungary until war broke out in 1914. He then went abroad and actively worked for its downfall, convincing Woodrow Wilson, among others, of the righteousness of creating Czechoslovakia. Although he is mostly remembered today for his honorable causes, some Austrians, in particular monarchists, accuse him of having "conspired against his sovereign," during the war years, and of discriminating against Catholics, Germans, and Hungarians in the newly formed Czechoslovak state. He's emblematic of the inner conflict of the decaying monarchy and its aftermath.

"I would think it would be a museum," I say.

"*Nejsou peníze,*" someone responds, jokingly using the Czech for "There's no money."

Looks like it will have to wait for a wealthy philanthropist, a community effort, or an economic boom.

Once on the bus, my friends and I exchange addresses, I hand out a few of my "Galloping Gypsy" entertainer's cards, and we Friend each other on Facebook.

Back in town, I stroll Martin's streets in the twilight, passing the angular white concrete Lutheran church. Here I once attended a commemoration of the Slovak Memorandum of 1861, signed on the square in front of the edifice. The petitioners hadn't insisted on independence, only cultural and linguistic rights, and decent treatment within the multi-ethnic state. Instead the Magyar aristocracy cracked down on the use of Slovak in schools, churches, and offices – especially after the Kingdom of Hungary had achieved its own autonomy with 1867's Ausgleich. But they didn't want to allow others that advantage. Such policies brought tensions to a boil. Franz Ferdinand, though, saw the Slavs as an essential "third pillar" of the monarchy. He hoped to put them on a par with the Magyars, with whom he had a reciprocal hatred. Hard to say what would've happened without that fatal shot in Sarajevo.

Whatever their historical sins, my next destination, the land of the Magyars, still fascinates me.

3

Hungary: Polysyllables, Paprika, and Pálinka

My van to Budapest is clean and comfortable. Hungarian driver István, in slacks and polo shirt, speaks English with ease. He chuckles at the cerulean-blue signs with white lettering announcing each town we pass through. "I just can't get used to zese long Slavic names."

"Most Slavs would find Somoskőújfalu unusual," I say, recalling the frontier railway station not far from here where I first entered the country in the wee hours one 1991 morning.

A smile twitches his lips. "From your pronunciayshun, you must know *some* Magyar."

"Took an intensive course in Debrecen. Been to Hungary many other times, too."

"So you know the nearest related language is Finnish. Our ancestors came from the Urals."

I nod. Hungarians romanticize their forbears as fearless horseman, early-medieval Danube-Basin conquistadors. Slovaks, on the other hand, picture the Magyars as ninth-century marauders who nearly destroyed the Slavs' "advanced, peaceful agrarian civilization."

As we wind down curves into Slovakia's southern flatlands, we pass signs with Slovak names of towns on top, Hungarian below.

"Here Magyar population is over twenty percent." István's short e's sound like the a in cat, typical of his countrymen. "So the signs must be bilingual."

"Yeah, and still nationalists here insist Hungarians call these towns by their Slovak names." I'm genuinely irritated at the thought, but also showing sympathy to get on his good side. I may need him later to get to Sarajevo. "As if English-only fanatics in America made everyone say 'The Angels' instead of 'Los Angeles.' 'Saint Francis' instead of 'San Francisco'."

"We have our nationalists, too." He snorts. "They complain today's Hungary is only '*Csonka Magyarország*'."

"Rump Hungary." I've seen the maps, like butcher's charts. The modern country, a third of its historical size, surrounded by the territories it lost after World War I: all of Slovakia, much of Romania, Croatia, and Serbia, and smaller chunks of Austria and Ukraine. A painful loss. I can sympathize, but revanchism sets neighbors on edge. At least István seems to get this point, unlike some of his compatriots.

Soon we're over the border, and on the road signs, the hačeks on Slavic consonants š, č, and ž have given way to Hungarian diacritics, like the distinctive double-acutes on the vowels ő and ű. We roll around hills north of Budapest, where the eastward-flowing Danube cuts south.

István drops me off at a hostel, where I check in, then launder six days' worth of dirty clothes, unsure when I'll have the next chance.

After dark, in the center of town, conversation and music occasionally break through grainy digital soccer-stadium cheers. World Cup matches blare from every café and bar – not really what I came here for. So I wander down a broad pedestrian thoroughfare with sandblasted walls on the adjacent buildings. All renovated in the past decade to give tourists and locals a more pleasing approach to the river.

It's much quieter on the Danube shore. Tourists on cruise boats lounge at dinner tables while passing under the string-of-pearl lights draped from the towers of the Chain Bridge. Buda Castle, bathed in pale-yellow floodlights, perches on the steep opposite bank. Franz Joseph was crowned Apostolic King of Hungary there. Legally, he'd held that title (and a long string of princely and archducal ones, too) since becoming Emperor in 1848. But the Ausgleich of 1867, which put Budapest on near-equal footing with Vienna, had required him to go through the coronation pageantry to please his Magyar subjects. He'd learned their tortuous Asiatic tongue from the age of twelve. But his wife, the elegant Sisi, known for her side-saddle equestrianism, long dark tresses and romantic spirit, became the family's biggest Magyarophile.

Franz Ferdinand, to the contrary, preferred Slavs to Magyars, especially after spending a none-too-happy military stint outside the western Hungarian town of Sopron, near today's Austrian border. He was fluent in Czech, but when Hungarian officers spoke their tongue, which he never mastered, he suspected them of mocking him in his very presence, while he was left to look on cluelessly, unsure what they were saying and unable to do anything about it. In 1914, in keeping with his aversion to everything Magyar, he chose to travel to Sarajevo via the Adriatic, while his wife Sophie went by train through Hungary. It's her footsteps I'll be retracing for this part of my journey. Roughly – due to recent flooding, I won't be able to make the entire trip by rail.

* * *

The following day at noon, I depart for the southern town of Pécs, my last overnight stop before Sarajevo. Although the train is supposed to traverse most of "Rump Hungary's" north-to-south axis, it has all the trappings of a local line: a chattering locomotive gushes diesel fumes. All four wagons behind it shudder.

Soon we coast gently from the hilly landscape around the capital into the more typically Hungarian plains. I flop my head back and take in the farmland, dotted by clusters of cypress and the occasional pole for raising the bucket from a well.

Two hours later, I have another *Grand Budapest* moment. "*Kell autobuszra átszállni*," the chubby conductor announces, resting pudgy hands on each seat as he saunters by.

"But we train direct, no?" I say in broken Hungarian.

"No, go bus now, train again later," his reply filters through. After further linguistic struggle, I gather there's construction on the line.

Funny no one mentioned this at Keleti Station when I bought my ticket. The promise of a direct route, of being able to stand and stretch while fresh air floods the carriage, crumbles. I grab my stuff from the overhead compartment, trudge around a dusty station with forty other passengers, like a band of refugees, to a waiting bus and stow my backpack and guitar below.

It's ninety inside the old Ikarus. The only windows that open are narrow sliding ones at top. My tee-shirt clings to my armpits, and I can smell the thirty other passengers. As the terrain rises, we wind around knolls and through valleys, the northern foothills of the Balkans. We have to move all our stuff again for the remaining twenty-minute leg by train. Why didn't they just take us the rest of the way by bus, having put us to so much trouble already?

In Pécs, I huff it with my "combat load," dodging VWs and Fiats in a major thoroughfare, then tramp ten residential blocks before arriving at a three-story, terracotta-roofed building with cream-colored stucco walls and begonias in every window. *Szent György Fogadó*, announces a circular sign with Gothic lettering and an image of the saint lancing the dragon. Would've made a nice addition to Ferdinand's St. George miscellany. Covered with sweat, feeling as if I've come from slaying a monster myself, I plop my stuff down inside the entrance.

"*Guten Tag! Ich bin Schiller, David,*" says a blond man behind the reception desk. "Are you Herr Nuckols, wis whom I spoke by phone earlier?"

"Yes, that's me." Hm, Schiller. Must be one of those ethnic Germans, who've lived in Pécs for centuries. No wonder the décor is so fastidious. Little ceramic vases of dried flowers dot the centers of red-and-white gingham tablecloths in the adjoining room. Spruce and pine dominate the furniture and bar counter. Schiller checks me in with all due haste, and I take a much-needed shower and doze in the AC.

Then I stroll to the town center, passing low-rise apartments with ivy-covered garden fences. Twin spires rise from the medieval town walls ahead. Near the top, these square brick towers have narrow columns in the middle of each face – the gaps serve as sound holes for the bells. Very Italianate – I'm making the transition to southern Europe.

Inside the ramparts, a fountain trickles and sprays, playing to my urge for peace, so I find a bench and gel to the rising and falling of the water-jets. Young Roma splay out on the grass in the afternoon breeze. A black dachshund dashes around. A shriek pierces the air as a tyke ventures near the cascade and gets sprayed. I wander down the square and take a photo from near the ground, over the heads of daisies, lavender and poppies, up the slope, toward the cathedral. Turns out it has four bell towers, two at each end, which fit symmetrically into the perspective. Nearby is an excavation display from Pécs's Roman period. It's rare for me to feel so in the moment *and* so steeped in the past.

Under the northern city wall, chatter beckons from picnic benches in a wine garden with lights hung like Christmas ornaments from trees and tarps – the latter to shade from the blazing June sun. I ask for a *fröccs*, a white-wine spritzer, the quintessential Austro-Hungarian summertime drink.

The bartender asks me something in rapid-fire Hungarian and, sensing my incomprehension, switches to English. "Do you want a long step or a short step?" He chuckles, knowing this literal translation doesn't go over so well. "We say 'short step' when you have one deci wine and one deci soda. It's a 'long step' with two deci soda."

"I'll have the long version." I need rehydration after all this walking.

Deeper in the heart of town, the Gazi Kasim Pasha Mosque presides over Széchenyi Square like a domed ziggurat, a reminder of the sixteenth- and seventeenth-century Turkish occupation. It's been converted into a church, as attested by the cross atop the crescent moon on the cupola, but its entrance still looks down the plaza at an odd angle, facing Mecca.

Farther along, a Trinity column and an equestrian statue, with an imperial-yellow city hall beyond, put me firmly back in Europe. The building's ornate copper domes, a familiar sight in Hungary, melt into the dark-blue twilight. Dozens of students sit on huge concrete planters. A guitarist playing Irish music completes the college-town feel.

I settle into a sidewalk table and order stuffed cabbage. Filled with rice and ground beef, it's as big as a burrito, and loaded with paprika. The generous topping of sour cream takes the edge off the spice. Inside, costumes on mannequins and posters lettered in type from numerous decades of the twentieth century, signal that I've stumbled onto a theater restaurant.

"Mind if I have a look around?" I ask the server.

"Here, let me turn the light on," she says, ushering me into a separate dining room with lattice woodwork like the chancel of a gothic church, complete with carvings of angels. Elsewhere, rough wooden beams, bulky booth dividers, almost like headboards on a Victorian bed, green gingham tablecloths, and turn-of-the-century costumes give things an early 1900s feel.

On another large square, several beverage stands cater to bustling crowds. With benches, tables, and a large screen, it's a communal living room for the summer's big entertainment: World Cup Football. I linger briefly, but am soon anxious for bed, worn out, but glad to have landed in such a friendly, cultured town.

* * *

I take a cab through morning drizzle to the Zsolnay Quarter, named for a family of Habsburg-era ceramics makers. Its old factory was nationalized under the communists, and later refurbished into a museum complex where craftspeople awl and stitch leather, and practice other trades for visitors to watch. The buildings' exteriors have walls, panels, and decorative molding in turquoise, mauve, yellow and other colors. Statues of griffins and Greek sphinxes with human breasts guard the front steps, while nymphs hover atop fountains and retaining walls. The restoration project won Pécs the European Capital of Culture title for 2010.

Generations of Zsolnays traveled the world collecting rarities such as Etruscan earthenware, and mastering classical Persian eosin glazing, which produces iridescent reds. The technique was little known in the West before the family discovered it, but they developed it further to render the greens, blues, and purples so characteristic of Art Nouveau vases. The method was also the source, I now realize for the first time, of colorful roof-tile designs I've admired on prominent Budapest buildings for nearly a quarter-century. The factory won major prizes at the Vienna and Paris World Expos in the 1870s, and by the early twentieth century was the largest ceramics firm in the Empire. Ferenc József, Emperor Franz Joseph, filled a whole page of the guest book with his Hungarian signature in 1880.

I browse and take photos of everything from European folk motifs to a Chinese girl drawing in a fishnet. The "Monumental Alhambra Vase" dazzles the eye with curly leaves, buds, and flowers topped by pointed arches, all in navy-blue, auburn, lime-green and bright yellow. But it's the Art Nouveau room—and the statuettes of hussars, with gold buttons and braid up and down their dolman jackets—that really remind me of the end-of-the-empire world I've come to rediscover.

After the weather clears, I ride a train past cornfields and fishponds to the nearby town of Villány. It's also a bilingual area, with a pale-yellow town hall marked *Városháza* and *Rathaus*. As the road steepens, hillside vineyards rise behind white-washed cottages lining the street, all of them *borozók*, or wine cellars, most with German names like Fritsch and Blum. At one, a proprietor enjoys a clear schnapps while laughing and making small talk with customers. The waiters invariably carry seltzer bottles, like it's part of the summertime dress code.

Inside the Gál *Pince* (cellar), a peasant with a gray moustache, wearing an open black vest, white linen trousers and shirt—with billowing sleeves and legs—reclines in a corner, next to a kerosene lantern in the middle of his heavy oaken table. His eyes hide beneath the shade of a black wool cap. Passed out from too much afternoon schnapps? No, he's just a mannequin. Out of the blue, a live man in bright red polo shirt welcomes me from behind the counter, where black-iron pruning shears from ages past cover the rough-hewn wallboards behind him.

Soon he has me trying *meggyes*, a grappa infused with sour cherry – and another flavor.

"Is there cinnamon in this?" I ask.

"Perhaps yes, perhaps no. The retsept is secret."

"Ah, recipe," I correct him, then savor the rest of the half-deci-
liter sample.

Just up the hill, at the *Hétfogás fogadó*, or Seven-tooth Inn, I
order a bottle of mineral water, then study the *pálinkalap*, a menu
of local schnapps: pear, elderberry, quince, even rose hip. The
smallest size, .2 dl, lets you sample several without getting drunk.
I choose apricot.

For a change from the usual Hungarian goulash and paprikash,
I order a cock stew with *turó*, Slavic-style curds. The cool dill and
sour cream nicely offset the sharp paprika. A glass of *kékfrankos*,
or "blue Franconian," comes chilled from the cellar. Named for its
violet hue and place of origin, it's common in Central Europe and
called *Blaufränkisch* in German and *Frankovka modrá* in Slovak.

Back in Pécs four hours later, walking back to the bed and
breakfast, I happen by a café-bar. Inviting, with locals of all ages
chatting and relaxing in wooden folding chairs on the sidewalk.
Inside, I spot the Polish liquor *Żubrówka*, with a bison on its apple-
green label.

"Have you seen *Grand Budapest Hotel*?" I ask the young barman
with his black crew cut.

"No, but I haf heerd of zis film."

"It takes place in a country called Zubrowka."

"Oh, like zis?" He pulls the bottle off the shelf.

I get him to pose with it for a photo, then ask for a shot. "Yes,
it's supposed to be a country somewhere in East-Central Europe.
The currency is called the klubek."

He laughs as he pours, shaking his head. "Probably Hungarian
forint strange to you."

I offer to buy him a drink. Since it's near closing, he accepts. "Here's to the Rrrepublic of Zubrrrowka!" I say. We clink and toss them back. It's only vodka with mildly herby infused bison grass, which gives it its Polish name. A disappointment after the plethora of fruity schnapps in Villány, but for symbolism it fits the bill. I pay with a crimson five-hundred-forint banknote, only a couple of bucks. Klubeks, indeed!

As I pick up my room key at St. George Inn's reception, a loud *pfshshshsht* comes from the mostly empty dining area. Four patrons are hanging out after hours, spritzing their white wines. Turns out they're Austrians. Seltzer bottles are starting to seem *de rigueur* here.

* * *

The next morning, I slip downtown and get a peek at the cathedral's ornate interior, which I'd missed before, but rain dampens any further touring. I ask a cabbie where to get lunch.

"*Szent György Fogadó*," he answers. "Best food in town."

So I'm already staying at Pécs's best restaurant. I take his advice – and a ride.

The rain patters on the awning over St. George's patio, as I savor my last meal in Hungary, the quintessential chicken paprikash, with cool-and-hot sour cream-and-paprika, and doughy, eggy galuska noodles, much like Bavarian spaetzle. The apple strudel desert, sifted with confectionary sugar, comes with bitter-sharp coffee, pampering my epicurean inner child.

It's a fine end to my stay in Pécs, which has kept me dazzled with its flavors and visual arts, as well as its friendliness. I'd like to stay longer, but I need to move on to my main goal, to make sure I'm there in time for the centenary.

A van should be coming soon to carry me to Sarajevo.

4

Getting to Sarajevo: Through a Flood Zone at the Speed of Z

At three PM, I'm still kicking back in my cushioned patio chair with a mug of frothy Borsodi. Hungary's breweries don't come close to Bohemia's, I suspect because Magyars are more dedicated to wine, but this will do for now. I'm just killing time, since my van driver has texted that he's running two hours behind. Headline-making floods in Bosnia have caused glitches in transportation lines, and this pricier option seems the most reliable way to get to Sarajevo in time for the centenary. Finally, after another hour, a late-model white van, clean except for bottom-panel spatter, pulls up outside the gate. Soon, we're zipping toward the next major route south.

With me sitting in the back seat, the driver keeps craning his neck to make eye contact, even as we merge with heavy traffic onto M60. "You don't have to look at me when we talk," I tell him nervously.

"Don't, uh, vorry. I uh, watching ze cars." Still, he keeps glancing between me and the road. Zoltan, younger than my earlier driver, is clean-shaven with close-cropped hair, but in tee-shirt and khaki shorts. And flip-flops – are they even legal behind the wheel here? A glass seltzer bottle with wire mesh rests in the console. They're so ubiquitous here, maybe I should get one, too, just to fit in. Nah. I have enough gear.

An hour later, we cross into Croatia, which has only signed an association agreement with the EU. So I have to show my passport for the first time since arriving in Prague.

Shortly after the border crossing, Zoltan stops for gas. Inside the convenience store, the clerk switches easily between Hungarian and Croatian, typical for the bilingualism of the area.

Zoltan pops in and stammers to her in English, "You, uh, have, uh, energy trink?"

When she replies in equally halting English, I intervene. "*De beszél magyarul*. But she speaks Hungarian." The two then communicate readily in their common native tongue.

Back on the road, Z says, "In communismoos, uh, no much work, much time for family. I born too late for zat." He goes on to tell me he worked eighty-hour weeks selling insurance, then quit for the sake of his wife and daughter. Hm, making up for lost time. And now, on the road, for my delayed pick-up. We barrel down a bridge across the gray Drava, broad and slow-flowing. With no traffic around, it's *sort of* safe to do ninety. I wonder if he sold auto insurance.

We stop for a quick supper in Osijek. At a McDonald's, he insists, to save time. I swear to myself it'll be the last time I eat fast food on this trip.

In the town center, pockmarked buildings recall the fratricidal wars of the nineties. Yet among the soot-stained facades, a plaque with gold lettering gleams with the name Josip Juraj (all J's pronounced like Y's) Strossmayer, a believer in the highest supranational ideals of the old monarchy. Born here in 1815, the Austrian archbishop spoke several languages fluently, and, as a patron of the arts and education, played a key role in the development of Croatian culture – at a time when most ethnic Germans looked down on Slavs. He, a Catholic, also advocated for the rights of Orthodox Serbs within the Habsburg Empire.

During Strossmayer's lifetime, Serbia gained its independence from the Ottoman Empire in 1817, as did other Balkan nations during that century (Lord Byron died fighting for Greece's liberation, for instance). The Kingdom of Serbia became the core around which the new Yugoslavia was formed at the end of World War I, officially known as the Kingdom of Serbs, Croats and Slovenes. Axis powers invaded in 1941, and an independent Croatia arose, a Nazi puppet state which later committed atrocities against Serbs, Jews and Roma. Reconstituted in 1945, Yugoslavia became known as the Socialist Federal Republic of Yugoslavia, ruled by the anti-fascist partisan from the World-War-II era, Marshal Josip Broz Tito. Tito, himself of mixed Croat-Slovene background, kept a lid on nationalist pressures by delegating power to the country's various regions: Croatia, Slovenia, etc. But after his death in 1980, relations among the Yugoslav ethnicities (which also included majority-Orthodox Montenegrins and Macedonians, Slavic-speaking Muslim Bosniaks and Albanian-speaking Muslim Kosovars), frayed steadily during the 1980s. War broke out in the early 1990s after Slovenia, Croatia and Bosnia declared independence from the federation. The dominant Serbs wanted to keep the country together, largely because there were sizeable ethnic-Serbian enclaves within Croatia and Bosnia that would face oppression as minorities in the newly sovereign states. Croats and Bosniaks, for their part, feared that Serbian areas would break away from their countries and form a "Greater Serbia." The desire to keep certain territories ethnically pure—in a land that for centuries had been a patchwork of nationalities—lead to acts of genocide on all sides.

In the twilight, Zoltan and I cross the Sava and slow toward the border. The official's shoulder patch is royal blue with white stars and a downward-pointing yellow triangle, the shape of Bosnia. He hands my passport back after a cursory glance.

But back on the road, a Cyrillic sign reads *Republika Srpska*. "What, we're in Serbia?"

"Yes."

"I thought we were going directly from Croatia into Bosnia."

"Yes," Z replies again.

Both can't be true, unless this is a tri-state area. If only I'd studied Balkan geography more closely before the trip. "So we're not in Serbia?"

"Yes."

"Yes, we are, or no, we're not?"

"We, uh, no in Serbia, we in, uh, Bosna."

Ah, yes, now I remember: this majority-Serbian zone was created under the 1995 Dayton Accords, which ended hostilities in the former Yugoslavia. The idea was to give the Serbs partial autonomy within Bosnia so they wouldn't tear out a chunk of the country and join Greater Serbia. And *Republika Srpska* is best left untranslated to avoid confusion with the Republic of Serbia, the fully autonomous country to the east. Of course, Zubrowka would have been a more distinct name.

The highways have been smooth, even at the speed of Z. But in Doboj (pronounced "DOUGH-boy"), we come to a single open lane, where we have to take turns with oncoming vehicles, advancing fifty yards, then stopping to let traffic from the opposite direction go by. Even at a creep, we bounce over rough, furrowed blacktop. The seat springs jostle my pelvis like a mechanical bull. On the roadside, gravel piles and steam rollers appear in our headlights. Z points to water lines on bungalows, left behind by the receding flood. A downpour starts – maybe another deluge is in store.

In serious Balkan territory now, we plunge down steep hills like a runaway truck. "Did I tell you, I used to be, uh, race car driver?" Zoltan asks.

Great. Guess he drove Formula Ones in flip-flops. Sure hope he knows how to handle a hydroplane, 'cause there's plenty of water at the bottom of these inclines.

Orthodox churches, with central cupolas and four smaller domes, well illuminated, stand out in the stormy darkness. In Republika Srpska, signs are in Cyrillic first, Latin characters second. But as we enter Bosniak turf, alphabets switch places. Minarets perch on the rough skyline like lighthouses for mountaineers. I visited Croatia once two decades ago on a choir trip, but I've never been this deep in the Balkans.

As we round the last hill north of Sarajevo, streetlamps glare by contrast to all the poor lighting we've seen. Tall, blocky concrete apartment buildings climb the steep slopes, as if resisting a mudslide to the river valley. Mosques stand everywhere. We exit the highway and glide through a neighborhood full of cottages. Packs of dogs wander the street, looking well fed for strays. Not the welcome I'd been hoping for at one AM. Zoltan pulls into the center of town. I'm relieved to recognize the bridges over the Miljacka from Google Earth.

We park, grab my things, and ask directions to my lodgings. Nobody seems to know. After twenty minutes of winding around an Ottoman-era bazaar full of shuttered tinsmiths' stalls, schlepping all my gear, we circle back and find *Pension Sebilj* a mere hundred feet from the van.

I pay Z at the reception, but he refuses a tip for carrying my backpack and guitar. I wish him well. As he saunters off, I wonder if this job really gives him much time with family.

At least *I* can stop worrying about time. I've got two days to spare before the anniversary.

5

Awaiting an Awkward Centenary

I slip out to have breakfast at a tidy wooden shack. Young women in headscarves cut slices of pastry from shallow, round baking sheets. They're like pizza pans, only they hold concentric coils of filo dough filled with beef sausage, feta cheese, or spinach. Here, the dish is called *burek*, and elsewhere in the Balkans, the Middle East and Central Asia, it is known as *borek* or *börek*.

"One, small, meat, burek," I order in Serbo-Croatian, learned in grad school ten years ago and now largely forgotten. A glass of sour kefir, a fermented milk product almost like a thick, drinkable yoghurt, completes the meal. Kefir originated in the Caucasus centuries ago and had become distributed throughout Russia by the early 1900s before catching on farther afield in the middle of the last century.

New country, new diet.

Hand-washing clothes back in my room, I'm reminded of Hungary's cuisine by the pungent paprika sweat on every shirt I wore in that country. It had literally been oozing from my pores. Variety is the spice, sweetness, meat, and cream of my life.

A blast of music startles me. A female voice quavers, accompanied by synthesizer chords in Arabesque minor, and a piercing reed instrument. I've line danced to similar music many times at Greek festivals in the U.S.: slow slow FAST-fast-fast, left right LEFT-right-left. A *davul* bass drum drives the caffeinated tango: *rom pom POM-pom-pom, rom pom POM-pom-pom.*

Welcome to the Balkans. I lumber up four steps from bathroom to bedchamber—an Ottoman feature, I suppose—and peer out a window. My room is above a bar/café serving beer to World Cup followers at ten AM. Guess I won't be taking any siestas here.

I trudge through a sprinkle of rain and find a tourist information office, despite the tiny lettering on its bag-brown storefront, nestled between a corner grocery and a Lotto outlet.

"I'm in town for the hundredth anniversary of the assassination," I tell the portly gray-haired lady behind the counter.

"Here is programme." She hands me a thin, slick canary-yellow brochure: *Sarajevo, Heart of Europe, 1914-2014.*

I flip to June 28. Several exhibits open that day, but no main ceremony. "Isn't there a commemoration at the time the shooting took place?"

"I suppose no. But here listed everysing happening."

I point to a Vienna Philharmonic concert for that evening. "Can I reserve a ticket?"

"It will be special concert in City Hall. Uh, invite only. Sorry."

"Thanks for the info." A bit discouraged, I step gingerly back outside.

I've spent three frustrating months researching events online: private clubs touring from Vienna to Sarajevo in period trains, peace groups holding symposia. But given the potential divisiveness, it's not surprising there's no central organizing committee. The Serbs of East Sarajevo are planning to unveil a monument to assassin Gavrilo Princip. In their view, the cataclysm he set in motion was justified by the destruction of the hated Habsburg Empire and the creation of Yugoslavia. Others find this lionization of a murderer distasteful.

The *baščaršija*, or bazaar, shuttered in the dark last night, now glistens in broad daylight. Westerners in shorts and sneakers gawk at copper- and tin-smiths' stalls. Two women in ankle-length black abaya squat to feed pigeons. Most women here don't cover even their hair. Backpackers in blond dreadlocks line up to fill water bottles at the marble base of a public fountain. Called a *sebilj*—like my accomodations—it's covered by a twenty-foot-tall kiosk of wooden latticework with a copper dome, a very Ottoman style. Behind it, the conical tip of a minaret pierces an overcast sky. On wooded slopes a mile away, houses cluster on terraced hillsides, terra cotta roofs matching those of the artisans' huts right in front of me. Not what I'd call the "Heart of Europe." But it does combine the charm of Italy—harmony between nature and architecture—with the exotic. Southern Europe meets Asia Minor.

Just down a pedestrian thoroughfare, at a smaller fountain—only marble with no lattice adornment—in the courtyard of the Ghazi Husrev-bey Mosque, worshippers remove sandals and perform ablutions. The *bey* in the name is an old Turkish word for chieftain. These faithful are Bosniaks, Slavic-speakers whose ancestors converted under Ottoman rule, many to avoid the *jizya*, the tax on non-Muslim subjects. Other Balkan Slavs remained Christian. I enter the gate and slip the gray cloth Sketchers from my feet. It's not prayer time, so there are more tourists than worshippers. In contrast to European Catholic churches which draw so many sightseers, the mosque is free of "idolatrous" statuary. The only wall decorations are green and red Arabic calligraphy and geometric designs; the space is bare except for carpets.

A neo-Gothic cathedral—which serves the city's Catholic Croats—looms over the street ahead, with twin spires, rose window, and statue of Jesus showing his Sacred Heart. Across the way is the Serbian Orthodox Cathedral. Although built in the nineteenth-century, the five-cupola structure follows a typical Byzantine layout, yet its bell tower is neo-baroque, a Western borrowing also found on churches in St. Petersburg, Russia.

I stop short at a newsstand, surprised at a tawny pseudo-antique map unfolded for display, with bold lettering in German: *Österreichisch-Ungarische Monarchie*, 'Austro-Hungarian Monarchy.' Bosnians don't look back on the old geo-political entity as bitterly as Serbs, but nations of the former empire rarely wax *this* nostalgic.

Suddenly, from a nearby square come strains of a military band playing the old Austrian *Kaiserhymne* by Haydn, better known today as the German national anthem. It must be a reenactment of Franz Ferdinand's arrival! I hurry down the block to catch it – only to see video of a different event on an outdoor café's widescreen. Germany has just won a World Cup match; it's a recording playing in a stadium in Brazil. The map back at the newsstand was meant to cash in on history buffs here for the centennial. I guess I'm one of the sappier ones.

In the evening I sip a *begova čorba*, the "bey's soup": chicken broth with carrots and okra, in a pewter bowl with matching lid, a sunburst handle suggesting royalty. My table overlooks a courtyard from a balcony; roofs slant this way and that, an M.C. Escher print *à la ottomane*. A black cat springs from an overhang onto terra cotta roof tiles slick with rain. He could spend his life in this city without ever touching the ground. But his fur looks sodden in this drizzle. Next comes the *hadžijski ćevap*, traditionally a kebab for one who's made the hajj to Mecca. A Catholic on a not-so-religious pilgrimage, I dig into the succulent veal strips stewed with onion and mushrooms, on a bed of rice pilaf.

I chew on the meat – and on the caprice of history. The Ottomans defeated the Byzantine Empire, taking Constantinople in 1453. By 1683 they were besieging Vienna. Only two centuries later, Turkey was the "Sick Man of Europe," forced to cede independence to Christian subjects: Greece, Bulgaria, Romania. In 1878, Bosnia became a protectorate of Austria. But it was a poison pill. The already-complex monarchy couldn't digest the mix of religions and nationalities. 1908's annexation of Bosnia by Catholic Austria enraged the Serbs, who had an independent kingdom of their own next door – and a huge ally in Orthodox Slavic Russia, which also sought influence in the region.

Perhaps conflict was inevitable, with or without an assassin's bullet.

* * *

After Friday morning's breakfast *burek*, I get a Turkish coffee at an outdoor café. It comes on a copper tray in a three-ounce copper cup, its handle twice as long as the mug is tall. The java bubbles on top. I ask a German backpacker at the next table, who seems comfortable with local rituals, "How do I go about drinking this?"

"Let it cool for a while, and scratch away the grains from the inside of the rim. Then pour your coffee on top of the sugar cubes."

"Ah, so that's why the sugar's in a little porcelain cup."

"Exactly. But you can drink it straight if you want."

I pour the black-brown coffee over one cube, but it's still more bitter than the strongest espresso I've ever tasted. I dip in the remaining sugar with a finger-sized spoon and watch it dissolve. Then sip again. Fruity-sweet Turkish delight, traditionally served on the side, offsets the beverage nicely.

After noon, I wander by a dusty old office where three men are singing and playing folk music on a guitar that's seen better days.

I poke my head in, self-conscious but determined to socialize with locals. "*Dobar dan.* Hello. Uh, nice song."

The guitarist, a heavyset man in black shirt and cap, smiles. "*Hvala.* Thanks."

Ice somewhat broken, I glance at a flimsy table set with trays of sliced cheese, cucumber, and tomato, and bottles of wine and schnapps. "What's the occasion?"

"Weekend. Court's over," says a wiry middle-aged man in a blue bailiff's uniform.

"Actually, he's only one works," adds a gray-haired fellow with black eyebrows.

The guitarist smiles again, revealing a gap between top front teeth. "Yes, we two are pensioners. Come in." He nods toward a chair. "Sit down."

Before I even reach my seat, the bailiff has poured me a shot of *rakija* – Balkan fruit schnapps. We introduce ourselves and clink glasses. I exhale after tossing it back. Must be a hundred proof, distilled from pear or plum.

But guitarist Neno abstains.

The bailiff smirks and gleams. "Excuse him, he's a strict Muslim," I understand him to say in his native tongue.

Neno smiles, grimaces, and says in English, "Really, it's because I am deeahbetic."

"And is Ramadan," Dragan the bailiff sputters. Apparently not his first drink of the day.

Neno takes a bite of sausage. "Yes, it's Ramadan. But as deeahbetic I must eat during day to keep up strength." He chuckles and passes the plate to me.

"No worry, is halal, all beef," Dragan goads once more, lighting a smoke.

So is he a Serb or self-deprecating Muslim? Whatever his religious background, I assume he's not practicing. I'm feeling antsy, afraid to join in this ethnic banter and make a stupid joke that truly offends. I can "go deep" in Slovakia, having lived there for years, but here I feel like a four-year-old wading into local culture. I also have to be my own lifeguard on a strange beach. Better to know where I stand, and remain close to shore, than to venture into even *potentially* shark-infested waters or undertow. I can return to this land for closer exploration another time.

Then I notice a poster on a wall in the next room. It's the

stern face and medal-laden uniform of Josip Broz Tito, the socialist Yugoslav dictator who kept a tight lid on nationalist aspirations – or 'unified the peoples,' as these guys would probably have it. I'll give him credit: he broke with Stalin, never joined the Warsaw Pact, even worked with India's Nehru asserting the Non-Aligned Movement of states that sided neither with the Soviets nor the West.

To my relief, Neno starts playing again. It's a descending chord progression, like those you hear from flamenco artists, or in "Stray Cat Strut." All three join in. Even with untrained voices, they have a knack for Middle Eastern vibrato, another legacy of Turkish rule, I assume. I can only pick out occasional words like *duša boli*, "my soul aches" – must be about lost love.

Neno launches into another tune, and soon Dragan is cackling at a line about Ustaše, Croatian fascists who committed atrocities against Serbs in World War II. Maybe this humor is a way of dealing with a painful past, but I'm afraid to ask.

After we share more food and drink, Neno explains that he's retired from the mountain rescue. He has several apartments for rent. Aha, that's why these guys are being so friendly. But I'm willing to consider a move to get away from the noisy *konoba* below my present room.

He escorts me over a bridge and up a hill, to a three-story building just beyond the Spanish Embassy. The flats are spacious, with balconies – even washing machines.

"I can come Sunday, my last day at the Sebilj," I say.

We shake on it.

Back down at the bank of the Miljacka, camera crews are setting up. I find a technician who doesn't look too busy and ask what's going on.

"The Vienna Philharmonic will be playing in the City Hall at six tomorrow. VIP only inside, but there will be a large screen out here for the public."

How appropriate, I think, looking across the river at the peach-and-mauve striped building with beige trim and decorative turrets along the top edge. It's where Franz Ferdinand made his last speech – flustered, following a bomb attack on his motorcade. His notes were flecked with the blood of a blast victim. After the stop at this *vijećnica*, he insisted on visiting the injured in the hospital. But at that point it was impractical to call in reinforcements to secure the route, as the soldiers who'd just been on maneuvers—the ones Ferdinand had inspected the previous day—were only then returning to their barracks in mud-splotched uniforms. So they drove on with a relative handful of police for crowd control.

I walk a few blocks along that old parade route to the Latin Bridge, where the driver made the fatal turn, unaware of the improvised plan to continue along the embankment to the hospital. As he put the car in reverse to correct his mistake, Princip stepped out of the crowd and got off a lucky pistol shot to the archduke's jugular. A second bullet struck Sophie, seated beside him. Both were dead within minutes.

From a mauve banner wrapped around two sides of the second floor of the Museum of Sarajevo, the old Schiller Café where Gavrilo Princip had lurked, the face of Franz Ferdinand looks south across the river, while Princip's, taken from a mug shot, looks west. *The street corner that started the 20*[th] *century*, reads the motto.

In a way, that's true. One could say that the nineteenth century began with 1815's Congress of Vienna, which ended the Napoleonic Wars and set Europe on the course of an unprecedented period of (relative) peace. It was easy for people to believe in inevitable progress. So when the war broke out, millions of illusions were shattered. But by one assassin's bullet?

Not exactly. Austrian generals and statesmen had long sought an excuse to deal a blow to Serbia, a perennial thorn in their side. There was the danger Russia would intervene on behalf of its client. German generals had been itching to invade the tsarist empire before it could complete a railroad project enabling it to dispatch troops rapidly to its western borders. Many events could have started the broader conflagration.

A young man with a violin case strapped over one shoulder, wearing black pants and pin tucked white shirt, apparently from a dress rehearsal for tomorrow's event, scans the inscription in a large stone at the base of the museum building. I read over his shoulder: "From this place on 28 June 1914 Gavrilo Princip assassinated the heir to the Austro-Hungarian throne Franz Ferdinand and his wife Sofia."

Inside stand mannequins of the couple arm-in-arm as he leads, taking a step down. Behind them is a blown-up grayscale photo of the vijećnica interior with its oriental columns, arches, and latticework – a replica of them leaving City Hall. In other vitrines in this one-room exhibition are photos of the conspirators and related objects, mostly copies or photos: travel documents used to get from Serbia into Bosnia, pistols, the cyanide flasks they were to drink to avoid capture, a tattered cover of the Bosnische Post announcing the deaths.

On one wall is yet another map of Austria-Hungary in peach and mauve – apparently favorite colors here. The museum immortalizes not just the city's most famous historical event, but also

Bosnia's entire Habsburg era. Only there's no hint of resentment, unlike what I've experienced in nearly every other country of the former monarchy.

Across the street, the Latin Bridge slopes gently upwards from each bank to the middle. It's covered in scaffolding. Police block the entrance as workers prepare lighting and stage equipment. All this preparation, but City Museum staff can't find me a detailed program. I'll have to abandon my American penchant for planning and leave things to fate.

Close to midnight, as I'm working on my blog back at the Sebilj, I hear music, obviously from a bigger sound system than the one in the bar below. Outside, lights glare on the bridge. I jog the two blocks down the street, just as another act comes on.

It's a man in black leather jacket with shaven head. His Balkan vibrato is much more polished than Neno's and Dragan's.

"Who is it?" I ask a bystander.

"Šaban Šaulić. He is most famous of Serbian folk-pop singers."

I can just make out the words *Verujem u ljubav* – "I believe in love." Good choice. I take some video footage and run back to my room to post it on my blog, then hit the sack.

6

Let the Celebrations, uh, Commemorations Begin

fter a late rising and a quick breakfast, I throw on the black suit I packed just for this occasion. No shorts on such a solemn morning. I hustle the two blocks to the corner, still not sure what events might be planned. Guards stand at the entrance to the bridge, but fortunately no one blocks the street, the former Franz-Josef-Strasse. Media crews with tripods and booms jostle with a hundred onlookers. A Prague journalist with hand-held recorder takes comments from fellow Czechs who've made the journey here. But there's no podium, no dignitaries—at least that I can identify—and no police cordon. Just a rope around a scarab-green 1911 Graf and Stift, a replica of the car. The original is permanently displayed in Vienna's Military History Museum.

A middle-aged woman waves an emerald flag with black lettering: *Associazione Storica*.

"I'm not sure I understand," I say hesitantly. "Who do you represent?"

"An historical association from Venezia. I do it for the memory of my grandfather. He fight in, uh, *la Grande Guerra*."

"The Great War."

"Yes. But he no die in the war. Still I do it for him."

In front of the museum is something resembling a restaurant *Please Wait to be Seated* sign. It's chained to knee-high iron stanchions, as if someone might try to steal it. I nudge my way through the crowd. It's a photo of a monument from 1951, created by a Serbian artist, footprints in relief on a sidewalk block at the spot where Princip fired. The caption says the sculpture disappeared in 1992. Gavrilo was a confused teenager at best, in my view. At worst, a criminal who refused to repent before dying of pneumonia in 1918 in a Bohemian prison (Theresienstadt, later infamous as a Nazi internment camp). Not someone who deserved a monument. But whoever—Croat or Bosniak—stole the sculpture committed both vandalism and a provocation, right as the Balkan wars were heating up.

"Any idea where this came from?" I ask a woman standing next to the display.

"I don't know," she says with a German accent. "Maybe local Serbs put it here."

She points at melted light-orange wax on the pavement below, the remains of Eastern Orthodox candles. Nobody had denied the Serbs the right to put this new marker here, but it also hadn't received any stamp of approval. Much like the unofficial, spontaneous gathering right now. After the assassination, Habsburg officials had erected a memorial to the slain couple (a photo of which I saw back at Konopischt) which remained until the end of World War I. It was removed shortly after Yugoslavia's creation and replaced by a plaque commemorating Princip and co-conspirators. The Nazis tore that down. Then came the footprints under Tito. What a struggle over historical memory on one small street corner.

"I'm from Munich but I'm living in Zagreb for three years now," the lady tells me. "Being so close, I just had to make the trip for the occasion."

"I lived in Slovakia for six years," I tell her. "So, I learned lots about Austria-Hungary. And I've been to several other formerly Habsburg countries, but this is my first time in Bosnia."

The graying German raises her eyebrows. "Did you know Karl von Habsburg spoke on the Latin Bridge last night?"

I gasp. The grandson of the last emperor, son of the last crown-prince, Otto von Habsburg, who died three years ago at the age of ninety-eight. "What time was that?"

"Shortly after midnight."

"Oh, no. I missed it by a few minutes." Damn, why did I spend all that time on blogging? Still, was I supposed to have waited all night for something, anything to happen?

Now all of us seem to be waiting for something to happen. Without any organization, how are we supposed to commemorate the event? Tourists take pictures of each other on the back seat of the antique convertible. Suddenly a guy with a curly black mop of hair and dark sunglasses, in black tee shirt and lightweight white jacket, steps out and sprays the narrow windshield with a squirt gun. A clownish thing of bright yellow and red plastic, so obviously a toy he wouldn't alarm security agents. Some people chuckle, others smirk.

"This isn't at all what I was expecting," I tell her. "Ever since high school, when I first learned of the assassination, I've thought of it as such a pivotal event. When I realized the centennial was coming up, it just seemed like destiny to be here. An encounter with history."

I recall a scene from Joseph Roth's *Radetzky March*, a novel about the decaying empire. Near the end, aristocrats hold a raucous party at a dissolute Polish nobleman's villa in today's western Ukraine. Late in the evening comes a telegram: *Heir to throne rumored assassinated in Sarajevo*. The waltzing stops. Someone plays Chopin's funeral march on the piano. Ah, yes, if I were organizing this event, that's what I'd have them play. Right at the time they died.

Finally, a couple much too young to be Ferdinand and Sophie emerges from the building. She in a white blouse—and leopard-print pants, ugh—carrying a white parasol, he in dove-blue officer's tunic, saber at his side. It's 10:45, right about the time of the assassination. Professionals and amateurs take still and video shots as they get in the back seat of the Graf and Stift.

An officer in modern Austrian uniform plays Count von Harrach, the lieutenant colonel who escorted the couple up until the shooting, standing on the running board to protect them. Three photographers monopolize the area near the car—as if they needed it with their zoom lenses. Others stand on tiptoes, holding cameras and cellphones overhead. "Harrach" grins at the attention.

A blond, bearded man dressed as a dervish—hip-length gray vest, collarless white shirt and long black whirling skirt—leans a simple wooden plaque with a picture of the murdered couple against the wall. "I'm Austrian," he tells curious journalists. "This costume is to show solidarity with Bosnian Muslims."

I wonder if some locals might take it as patronizing.

One man lays a wreath with a broad silver ribbon saying "peace" in six languages. Another wreath, black and gold, reads *In ewiger Errinerung*—in eternal memory—followed by *Viribus Unitis* and *Katharsis Oesterreich*. I ask the German woman what it means.

"*Viribus Unitis* means 'with forces united.' The personal motto of Franz Joseph. And the name of the dreadnought Franz Ferdinand sailed across the Adriatic. It also took his body back. But I have no idea about this Katharsis Oesterreich."

Behind the car, a man chants through a megaphone "Down with nationalism!" It's an Austrian monarchist in black-and-yellow necktie, the colors of the House of Habsburg.

I join the dozens milling about inside the City Museum. In hushed tones, everyone watches an old black-and-white European movie scene of the shooting.

Around eleven-thirty, having marked the occasion as best as possible, the crowd thins.

I drift away, too, down to the City Hall, hoping to get more info on the evening concert, maybe wangle a ticket or invitation by some odd chance, or even run into a Habsburg. Near the entrance, I wince at a granite plaque chiseled in English, clearly aimed at international visitors:

ON THIS PLACE SERBIAN CRIMINALS
IN THE NIGHT OF 25th-26th AUGUST,1992 SET ON FIRE
NATIONAL AND
UNIVERSITY'S LIBRARY
OF BOSNIA AND HERZIGOVINA
OVER 2 MILLIONS OF BOOKS, PERIODICALS
AND DOCUMENTS VANISHED IN THE FLAME

DO NOT FORGET,
REMEMBER AND WARN!

Given the awkward correction in "millions"—there's only one L in the Bosnian word—it must have been done hastily, for this occasion. The building is re-opening today after lengthy renovations following war, financial difficulties, and bureaucratic snafus, so I can understand the defiance. But given the baiting tone, I can't blame the Serbs for boycotting the event.

Serbia suffered the brunt of demonization in the wars that engulfed the former Yugoslavia, but there's plenty of vengefulness to go around in the Balkans. It seems Catholic Croats and Muslim Bosniaks get along much better with each other than either do with Serbs – which may seem ironic, since both Croats and (Eastern Orthodox) Serbs are Christians. Franz Joseph deserves some blame for this strange split. Once Bosnia came under Catholic Austria's sway, he added Islam as an official religion of the Empire, but not Eastern Orthodoxy, only adding fuel to smoldering Serbian resentment.

Posters in Plexiglas on metal legs stretch for a quarter mile along the south bank of the Miljacka, an exhibit called *Making Peace*, sponsored by the International Peace Bureau. In one, a statue of a revolver with knotted barrel stands in front of New York's UN Headquarters, a work created by a Swedish artist in the aftermath of John Lennon's killing. Another quotes Eisenhower in Bosnian, Serbian, and English: *This world in arms is not spending its money alone – it is spending the sweat of its laborers, the genius of its scientists, the hopes of its children.* Then comes a lovely photo of the bridge in Mostar, Bosnia, arching fifty feet over the river. The caption says the original was built in 1556 by the Ottomans, only to be destroyed in 1993 by fighting between Catholic Croats and Muslim Bosniaks. So it wasn't just the Orthodox Serbs versus everyone else. The structure was rebuilt in 2004. Much like its cousin here in Sarajevo, it slopes gently up two sides to a point, like two arms reaching to one another. Its reconstruction seems a reconciliation of sorts. Such a pity that even the oldest bridges fall victim to wartime desperation to deny the enemy an easy crossing.

In the National Museum, a now-permanent exhibit on the siege of Sarajevo again seems less than conciliatory towards the Serbs. It is perhaps understandable, given that the blockade lasted from 1992 to 1996, and two Serb commanders were later convicted of crimes against humanity.

Walking back toward the town center, I notice bullet holes in the masonry of apartment buildings whose balconies doubtless provided good sniper positions. Some holes still gape, others are filled with patching plaster but haven't been painted over even after twenty years.

An Italianate bell tower down the street beckons. It's St. Joseph's, a sandstone-brick church that would even fit in urban American surroundings. A bulletin board outside calling for aid to victims of recent flooding reassures me Christian charity is not lost in this sea of ethnic tension. The notice is from the downtown Franciscan monastery; presumably they're helping Muslims and Orthodox as well as Catholics. I swing open a paneled door to polished marble floors, gleaming in sparse light from modest stained-glass windows.

As I pass up the aisle, a frail elderly lady addresses me. "*Dobro došli!* I haven't seen you here before." I've never had such a welcome in a European church.

"I'm visiting, from America," I say in halting Croatian.

She takes a hymnal from the back of a pew. It's bound in bright-red cloth, with glossy, multi-colored ribbon markers. She turns the spotless, smooth pages. "Finally, we have the whole liturgy in *our* language."

In Croatian, not Serbo-Croatian, she means. To me it's like declaring Australian a separate language from English, but in the former Yugoslavia, even Montenegrins have taken pride in codifying their own specific tongue. Some argue that Serbo-Croatian was an artificial nineteenth-century creation, cobbling together several different dialects at a time when the South Slavs had no official language of their own. Here, it's taken time and money to get these new prayer books finally printed, and they don't seem to have spared any expense.

But why *our* language? "I'm a foreigner," I repeat.

"Mass starts at five." She's not quite all there, doesn't register that I'm not a Croat. Perhaps suffering from Alzheimer's?

It's a quarter past, so I look at side altars, then kneel to pray. The priest appears during the opening hymn, and I follow the liturgy in the pristine hymnal.

After Mass, I feel moved, on this day, to add special prayers. For peace. For the souls of the departed, including Franz Ferdinand and Sophie. For all those, of any faith, who lost loved ones in the Balkan wars. Even for the soul of Gavrilo Princip. Even if he was remorseless, he was, to be charitable, pursuing the aspirations of his nation. (Even in authoritarian Austria-Hungary, basic law forbade the death penalty for anyone under twenty, regardless of the crime.) Still, only God can judge a soul, and it's gravely sinful to desire the eternal damnation of any human. "God have mercy on them all," I say, and rise from the kneeler.

Back in broad daylight, I scurry the whole mile to the spot across the river from City Hall. Hundreds of people of various ages, most standing, some reclining on picnic blankets, watch the ten-by-fifteen-foot screen. I'm just in time.

A red-headed Clemens Hellsberg, Vienna Philharmonic president, says with quavering lip, "It is more than a concert that brings us together in this building, it is a passionate plea for reconciliation."

The sandy-haired but graying conductor Franz Welser-Möst climbs the podium and begins the Bosnian national anthem. A few of those gathered sing, but most are foreigners. Smiles spread across faces as Welser-Möst announces Joseph Strauss's "Olive Branch Waltz," composed in 1866, when, in his words, "the Austrians were war-weary" following the Austro-Prussian War. Later, Haydn's old "Kaiser-Hymn" gets substantial applause, though it was diplomatically risky to play the old Austro-Hungarian anthem. But I don't see any angry faces. After an hour of Viennese favorites, the concert ends with "Ode to Joy." It's an abbreviated, purely orchestral arrangement of the final "Chorale" movement to Beethoven's Ninth. A pity there's no chorus, as in the symphony, but I join a few others standing nearby, who, teary-eyed, sing the line "*Alle Menschen werden Brüder.*" All people become brothers. Amen.

And yet, as hundreds file peacefully from the little park to the bridge, I spot another sign of discord. Protesters hold signs saying "I am Gavrilo Princip." Some wear masks of his face—the same mug shot that appears on the banner outside the museum. Are they Serbs, far-left activists, or both?

"What's your point?" I ask a frowning young woman, probably a college student.

"They spent two million Euros on this event." It's a common theme among the group's placards. "Bosnia has EU association contract. Rich Westerners will buy out everything. Leave us nothing."

I can understand her point, given how Britain's TESCO and other supermarket chains have acquired near-oligopoly status in other formerly socialist countries that have joined the Union. And the EU *could* be seen as a renewal of the old Austria-Hungary. After all, Otto von Habsburg, the last heir to the throne, had worked for years, both as Euro-Parliament chair and in retirement, for inclusion of former East Bloc countries—many of his family's old dominions—in the EU. In a way, it is a repetition of history. One that many Serbs just don't cotton to.

A wiry young man next to her quickly adds, "Next comes NATO. And you see what CIA is doing, supporting Ukrainian fascists."

I purse my lips and take a deep breath, considering his view without agreeing or disagreeing. What he's saying contains *only an element* of truth. Following the Maidan Revolution that overthrew Kremlin-friendly Prime Minister Viktor Yanukovich, Arseniy Yatsenyuk became Ukrainian prime minister in February 2014. Some twenty percent of his cabinet were nationalists. Many people in Ukraine honor the legacy of Stepan Bandera, whose Ukrainian Insurgent Army fought for independence from the Soviet Union toward the end of WWII – not surprising given that Stalin killed four million of them in the state-imposed famine of 1932-33. But the UPA itself ethnically cleansed as many as a hundred thousand Poles—and smaller numbers of Jews and Roma—from western Ukraine. Now, in 2014, Putin followers tend to look at the entirety of Yatsenyuk's government as a gang of Banderites; never mind that eighty percent of his cabinet are normal, center-right politicians. The problem is that Yatsenyuk simply had to give some posts to the far right in order to cobble together a majority coalition.

As for the CIA, who knows for sure what role they've played in Ukraine. But there are plenty of indications that they and other Western intelligence organizations funded, trained and armed the Kosovo Liberation Army in the late nineties, when some U.S. politicians were bragging about the support and others were calling the KLA a terrorist organization. The Kosovo region, which later detached from Serbia, consists mainly of ethnic Albanians (non-Slavs), called Kosovars, and a significant minority of ethnic Serbs. But the region is sacred to the latter as it was the scene of a pivotal battle between them and the Turks in 1389. The two armies nearly wiped each other out, but the Ottomans eventually sent in more forces from their vast empire and took over the territory. The

Serbs nonetheless commemorate their ancestors' heroism – the most famous poem in their language is "The Battle of Kosovo Polje." So when Kosovars began clamoring for independence in the 1990s, it set off alarm bells among the Serbs, including fears the Kosovars would join up with a "Greater Albania." There has long been tension between Serbs and Kosovars—even Tito had trouble keeping it down—so it was a major humiliation when the U.S. recognized Kosovo independence in 2008. Given Serbia's status as a client state of Russia, Putin also took it as a poke in the eye.

It's all so messy I decide to avoid the unpleasant discussion with the local Serbs, and instead head back to my room at the Sebilj.

After posting footage of the philharmonic's performance on my Galloping Gypsy website, I lumber through the baščarija in time to claim a small sidewalk table just as a couple leaves. I order a dish of peppers and tomato stuffed with ground beef and rice. Its savory paprika and cool sour cream, complimented by a dryish red wine from somewhere in the nearby hills, have me thinking of Pécs and Budapest. Or maybe it's the petite brunette and man in blond ponytail, in their late twenties, at the next table. I listen intently – yes, they are speaking Hungarian.

I try to think of how to start up a conversation when their food arrives. "*Jó étvágyot!*" I say. "*Bon appétit!*"

"*Köszönjük*, Thank you," she says, followed by a torrent of Magyar.

I hold up a hand. "Sorry, my Hungarian isn't that good."

"Your pronunciation is great, though."

"I learned it from the Magyar minority while living in Slovakia, and improved it at a summer program in Debrecen. Anyway, I'm here doing travel blogging."

"Oh, nice. I'm a reporter covering a story. I'm Edita, by the way, and this is László, my cameraman and photographer."

We all shake hands. I mention my disappointment at the poor event coordination.

"I have the same problem." She grimaces. "Even though I know Serbo-Croatian – that's why I got this assignment. Also, I spoke with other journalists in Sarajevo for the occasion. Everyone is frustrated at the lack of info."

"But of course, the Bosniaks, Croats, and Serbs all have a different take."

She nods.

So it wasn't just bad planning on my part. We exchange business cards, then clink glasses.

"*Egészségünkre!* To our health." I may be a freelancer with no assignment except his own blog, but I feel we're in this together.

Later in the evening, I watch more performances from the Latin Bridge on a large-screen TV atop a trailer. At least organizers did that much for the public. A theater troupe reenacts the plight of displaced persons during the Balkan Wars of the 1990s. A Cossack choir follows: men in furry hats and billowy uniforms with bandoliers sing full-throated Russian harmonies to an accordion. The streets are more crowded than ever now—this is a truly non-controversial event. People milling about under the willows and poplars speak mostly Bosnian-Croatian-Serbian; a number of women are in headscarves. A lone tourist now, I still feel remarkably calm, unhurried. I'm also unworried, about getting mugged or pickpocketed, that is. Edita told me Sarajevo has one of the lowest crime rates in southern Europe.

7

Hiking, Shisha, and a Charming Bosniačka

After I settle into my new lodgings at Neno's place Sunday morning, he takes me out of town for hiking. Soon, we're in his white early-nineties VW Golf, chugging up a steep, curvy highway headed eastward into Republika Srpska. Road signs in Cyrillic take precedence over Latin script. Twenty minutes later, we leave the highway for a bumpy gravel lane. He stops and idles at a stream lined by stone walls, where water gushes from little concrete troughs, a crude fountain.

"That's an ancient source, five hundred years old, minimum," he says. "Pure water, you can fill bottle."

I hesitate before getting out. Streams can look fresh yet contain nasty bacteria, or so I've read. But Neno is a mountain rescue guy. Trusting his knowledge, I guzzle some, clear and cool, then refill.

We continue to a cabin run by Neno's friends. Serbs, judging from the Orthodox icons on the paneled walls. Other decorations include photos of guests skiing and hiking, but curiously, they're taped around a chart illustrating fifteen varieties of poisonous mushrooms.

Neno has me sit on a balcony where he's prepared a lunch of burek and tea. I munch away on the doughy goodness. The tubes of filo are stuffed with meat and spinach and wound into a spiral before baking. The bumps and grooves remind me of a quilt; it's browned on the outside, flaky inside. I gaze over fields of tall grass and wildflowers, with three wood-and-wire fences stretching to dark evergreens in the hills beyond. Neno has calves like a linebacker, so you might think he'd be leading me on the trail. But with his diabetes, he takes it easy these days. Instead, he introduces me to my guide, Bojan, who carries trekking poles, like ski poles on summer duty.

Soon Bojan and I are marching up rough trails among under-growth of pine saplings and ferns. He sets a swift pace, then pauses to allow me to catch up.

Offering a quick break, he mimes a photographer. "*Slikati? Slikati?*"

I hand him my digital, and he snaps one of me sitting on a boulder.

Using simple nouns and infinitives, he points to hoof prints in half-dried mud. They could be deer tracks, or chamois for all

I know. We enter a gently sloping clearing, where my ankle-high shoes go *shlup, shlup* in water-logged soil, nearly pulled off my feet by suction. Thistles scratch my calves. Now I see why he's wearing long pants and rubber boots in the eighty-five-degree heat. He's black-haired but graying, pushing fifty like me, though in better shape. A lean, tan outdoorsman.

"*Slikati? Slikati?*" He sweeps his arm toward the surroundings. Limestone crags rise sharply beyond sixty-foot pines. As we ascend further, the trees thin, and the karst cliffs come into plainer view. Bojan points to caves in the side of the hills. "*Banditi. Dvjesto, tristo godina.*"

I take it to mean, bandits hid there two or three hundred years ago. Then I spot a red-blue-and-white Serbian flag, about four by six feet, painted on a vertical surface. I'm guessing the graffitist hung from the cliff above. That took guts. Who'd dare get up there and remove it now? Bojan makes no comment; I decide not to ask his ethnic background. Too much controversy here I still don't understand. My Sherpa seems like a nice guy. That's all that matters now.

Soon it's time to descend, but the path is over fist-size stones which have apparently chipped off the cliffs and now are making a slow-motion, centuries-long rockslide. A talus slope. The piles are a foot deep – and it's a forty-percent grade.

Suddenly my South Slavic improves. "*Ne možeme iti tako, kako sme došli?*" Not entirely grammatical, but enough to communicate: "Can't we go back the way we came?"

He shrugs, eyes gleaming behind wire rims. "Don't be afraid. I'll help. You have to see the vista beyond."

He beckons me on, has me put a hand on his shoulder while he holds me up by an armpit. The rocks crunch as he inches sideways downhill, stabilizing himself with a pole. I follow: right foot down a bit, then the left catches up. We scrutinize our footing every bit of the way. A pebble comes loose and bounces fifty feet downhill. If we start sliding where will we stop? I warily calculate each step, looking for the most stable clusters of rock. Eventually we start moving in sync as he calls the steps: "*Iiiii JEDAN, iiiii DVA*, aaaaand ONE, aaaaand TWO."

Wait a minute – is this how Balkan line dancing started?

Stones scoot out from under my shoes, but Bojan, amazingly solid with his wiry frame, catches me just as I'm about to lose balance. Finally we get past the treacherous part, and he lets me take a breather. I can stop looking at my feet. Now, a gap in the trees opens up, ridges spread out beyond, one after the other, for thirty miles. That's the view he was talking about.

Bojan points at a lesser crag and says in a hoarse whisper. "*Tamo, tamo.* There, there."

A dark brown mountain goat eyes us from a hundred yards away. So those are the hoof prints we saw earlier.

Back at the cabin, Neno pays Bojan. On the ride back to Sarajevo, he brings up the price I'm paying. "For tings like dis, two meals and laundry, fifty euros a night is fair, no?"

I'd rather know prices up front, but this is a bargain. So much included. We shake on it.

BAM! A pothole makes the car bounce.

"*Jebam piču tve mati!*" exclaims Neno. Something involving genitalia.

We didn't have these problems in the eastbound lane.

BAM! Another.

"*Jebam piču tve mati!*" This time I decipher: I fuck the cunt of your mother. Yeah, I've heard Balkan cussing can get awfully graphic.

Greeks have an expression like "I fuck your Virgin Mary." Whatever you hold sacred. Neno, thank God, is just cursing at the road.

I don't know what Islam says about foul language, but I'm guessing my host isn't that observant. His friends that I met two days ago were probably old army buddies of his. I think back to Father Živojin, the Orthodox priest from whom I learned Serbo-Croatian at Ohio State. At an end-of-quarter party, someone brought bottled beer, but no one had openers.

"Give me two of them," the cleric in collar said. He turned them end-to-end, hooked the rims of the caps under each other, and yanked. One came open, no glass broke, and only a tiny drop of suds wet his black trousers.

"Father, where'd you learn that trick?" someone asked.

"In the Yugoslav army, of course."

Ah, yes, the army that "turned boys into men," while defending only their own borders, never getting into conflicts. Until the country came unraveled in the early nineties, that is.

Back at the apartment, I open a beer stashed in the mini-fridge. Then I notice a fruit juice bottle, empty except for an inch of clear liquid in the bottom. I unscrew the aluminum cap and sniff. Ah, the sharp fumes of distilled pear, rakija. Neno isn't such a strict Muslim he wouldn't provide schnapps for his guests.

A cannon blast resounds from across the river, as it does every evening in Ramadan to announce Iftar, the end of the day's fasting. I step onto my balcony in the twilight. Downtown, I could make out an occasional call from a single minaret over the city noise. But here they waft from every mosque on the hillsides. Raspy tenors sing drawn-out lines in longing, melodic minor scales. Most issue from loudspeakers, probably recorded, and the initial impression is eerie, like air raid sirens. But I quickly remind myself of where I am, and the surround-sound has me feeling firmly in Islamic space, even as I kick back in a deck chair and drink a double-fisted toast of beer and schnapps. A tolerant Islamic world, this is.

* * *

In the morning, Neno drives through drizzle to a hill in the northeast so I can see citadel ruins. When a break in the rain comes, I climb among the foundations and crumbling brick walls. The fog clears, opening a view of City Hall, Latin Bridge, and the cozy neighborhood across the river where I'm staying. But soon the rain starts again. We get back in the car and wind slowly through this city quarter, past Muslim cemeteries full of obelisk headstones, topped by winding knobs like pasha's turbans.

Then we come to twin stone towers, over two centuries old, I would guess, linked by an old section of city wall. *Museum Izetbegović* reads a sign.

"He was the first president of independent Bosnia and Herzegovina." Neno sets his parking brake but makes no motion to get out. He's stopped for a truck backing out of a driveway in the hilly streets. He shakes his head. "Izetbegovic was one crazy fuckrrr."

I figure the old president couldn't have kept his nose very clean in the civil war, even if there wasn't enough evidence to drag him off to the International Criminal Court. But before I can ask about possible war crimes, my host continues his rant. "You know why you can't see Sarajevo Haggadah in National Museum?"

The fourteenth-century manuscript, a text for the Passover Seder, was brought here by Sephardic Jews who'd fled to the Ottoman Empire from the Spanish persecutions. A great symbol of Muslim tolerance contrasted with a shameful chapter in Catholic history. I'd wanted to see it two days ago, it was right across a grassy square from the Historical Museum. But the National Museum was closed.

"Why?" I ask timidly.

"Ha! Closed for renovation. Who knows how long? No money, they say. But they spend millions on Izetbegović. You write that in your blog! Our fucked-up city government!"

Though I know nothing of local politics, I'm glad to see my host takes pride in this piece of Judaica. The truck goes on its way, and Neno drives up another hill, to a bar-café-restaurant overlooking town. It's full of porches and balconies, windows everywhere give it a light feel despite the dreary weather. Three-foot hookahs stand between knee-high tables. We sit down on cushions right by the windows, next to two women and a man. The younger female has blond hair pulled back in a ponytail, flawless light bronze skin, thick lips accentuated by red gloss. She's a little taller than my five-foot-nine, but I wouldn't let that intimidate me. Still, the guy's probably her boyfriend. The waiter brings them bricks of shi-sha, the flavored tobacco that became so popular among the college crowd in the 2000s. Soon they're puffing from the long hoses.

Neno gets a tea. I order an orange juice.

"I've only smoked this once before, but I'd like to try again." I had it once in grad school at Ohio State, back when it was a new trend. Now, ubiquitous off-campus hookah bars have health experts alarmed at the popularity of the vice.

Neno calls the *konobar* over. I choose cherry from among the flavors, and I catch the young woman's eye as she exhales.

She smiles. "You're from America?"

"Yes."

"How do you like Sarajevo?"

"Wonderful, I feel so relaxed. Now that I've been here six days."

"How long are you staying?" Her English is only slightly accented.

"Leaving tomorrow. I have to get back to Prague sometime." I recount my aim of traveling around the former Austria-Hungary. Her thin sweater, slung over a blouse, seems a moderate Muslim nod to modesty. The mauve top—yes, that color again—offsets her pinkish-red slacks, which leave only well-turned ankles exposed. Even the slight dimples in her cheeks give me a charge.

She introduces herself as Naida; the other two are her brother-in-law and sister. Maybe she's not taken.

My tobacco plug arrives, and the waiter sets it in the bowl with glowing charcoal to keep it going. I feel giddy after just a few drags. Probably more nicotine than my typical quarter-pack-a-day cigarette intake. A relaxing buzz. Also a social stimulant. Or is it the girl?

"Are you sure this is only tobacco?" I chuckle.

"You never can be sure," Naida answers playfully.

"Ha, ha. Maybe we can trade for a moment." The ends of the tubes have little cones, removable plastic tips, for hygienic sharing. We switch, and I try her tart apple, looking up to catch a flirtatious gleam in her dark brown eyes. With any luck, we could spend more time together. Maybe I should extend my stay.

But the three soon get ready to leave. We take pictures of the five of us around the hookah. Naida leans in close, warm against my shoulder. Then she stands and pulls out her iPhone. "Can we be friends on Facebook?" I give her my card, she looks me up and taps the screen. "There, I just sent the request."

Then we go our separate ways. Oh, well.

* * *

The weather clears in the afternoon, and I slip out to Ilidža, the nearby spa-town where Franz Ferdinand and Sophie spent their final nights together. In the resort section, expansive lawns are intersected by brick walkways, and fountains spray as people chat at outdoor cafes. I find the Hotel Bosna, where the couple stayed, hosting a gala dinner the night before their deaths. It's an unassuming building: cream-colored façade, mostly rectangular windows, taller arched windows on the ground floor. An A-shaped roof towers over the rest of the four-story structure. This is where Franz Ferdinand arrived and met back up with his wife after their separate journeys. I've been following *her* path since Budapest, and now I begin retracing *his* journey, mostly in the opposite direction – unless you count the return trip to Vienna made by his corpse.

In the evening, I settle into a sidewalk restaurant for a last plate of *ćevapčići* , beef and strong onion. I hang out in downtown till eleven, alone yet not alone, watching faithful Muslims coming from late-night prayers, strolling the streets past beer drinkers like myself. I've not seen anyone drunk here, or loud. Nor any of the pornography stands you'd find in Prague or Vienna. Maybe that's part of the coexistence, the avoidance of offense to the religious. So it's hard to fathom the violence of two decades ago. Could it still be simmering beneath the surface? I hope not.

On the way back to Neno's building, passing under a rain-streaked oriel window, I imagine there are cushions to lounge on inside. I wish, for a moment, to be a cat curled up on one. I feel like being lazy and lingering indefinitely in Sarajevo. There's still much to see. And Naida.

Eh, she probably has a boyfriend. If it's meant to be, I'll see her in another couple of years. Leave it to the Fates. I have a bus to Mostar and Dubrovnik in the morning. And a comfy room up the hill – for this last night.

8

Dubrovnik and Split in Adriatica

In the morning, Neno drops me off at the bus station.

He gives me his card. "If your friends coming to Sarajevo, send them to me."

"I sure will. I really enjoyed the stay."

We say goodbye with a firm handshake.

I get a ticket to Dubrovnik, Croatia with a two-hour stopover in Mostar, the Bosnian town with the famous bridge reconstructed after being blown up in the 1990s. It's been on my bucket list for years.

As I look for my platform a fiftyish bleached-blonde blurts out in accented English, "Excuse me, sir, can I ask you something?"

"How should I know?" I mutter in Slovak and keep moving brusquely, a ruse to get her to leave me alone. If I'm so obviously a foreigner, why would she want my help? Seems suspicious, likely the opening volley of a scam.

Feeling vulnerable as a lone traveler, I hand my guitar and backpack over to the driver and take a window seat just above the compartment where he stows them.

Soon we zip along a turquoise river lined by poplars, willows, and cottages, restoring my serenity. But I'm jolted back into vigilance when a twelve-year-old girl across the aisle holds her smart phone at her hip and angles it at me. *Shshlunk* goes the shutter. Why would she want my picture? A pre-teen infatuation for a total stranger? Or am I the mark in some scam?

I'm relieved when she gets off in Mostar's outskirts. A man, apparently her father, gives her a kiss on the temple as she descends. Okay, I'm being paranoid.

At the station, I check my guitar and large bag and saunter into town with tablet and other essentials in a computer bag hanging from my shoulder – and tucked firmly under an arm. Pockmarked brick walls, and one hollowed-out building remind me once again of the civil war. As does a Muslim cemetery sloping down to the street, with death dates in the early nineties.

I wander past flocks of tourists and souvenir stalls on the meandering alleys near the *Stari most* or Old Bridge which gives Mostar its name. I hurry down the main drag to a different, modern bridge, which gives me a great photo angle on the old one. The latter rises at twenty-degree angles to a peak in the middle. Wooded hills,

Italianate bell towers, and minarets form the background. Then I jog, anxious about time, back along the other bank. I find a restaurant nestling twenty feet above the Neretva. For just fifteen bucks, I get lunch, wine, and a view of *Stari most.*

At its high point, a lean, dark-haired man in black Speedos leans on a tall stool as Asian tourists pass in both directions.

"Who's that?" I ask the waiter.

"Oh, he diver. When someone pay him enough, he jump."

My God, the water hardly looks deep enough for him to take the thirty-foot plunge without breaking his neck.

But even after my forty-five-minute meal, he's got no takers. I trudge up the incline, with its cinder-block-sized rough stones, and pass him myself. Then traipse down the other slope and toward the station, melancholic at having crossed off a destination with little to show but photos.

Still, I've seen things Franz Ferdinand would have seen and tasted the sorts of things he would have enjoyed here. *The Telegraph* published an article online just before the centenary saying that Franz Ferdinand "received a rousing reception in Mostar, the first major Bosnian town he came to..." I don't have any details on just where that was, but at least I can mark off one of his stops. For this part of his Bosnian journey, he sailed up the Neretva river on a smaller vessel called the Dalmat, after disembarking from the battleship Viribus Unitis at the Neretva Delta, where the river meets the Adriatic. Arranging a visit to that swampland, full of mandarin trees, the article says, is a bit out of reach for me. My next destination will have to be the more "mundane" city of Dubrovnik.

At the station, I retrieve my guitar, Emilia, and my backpack, relieved they haven't been stolen. Really, I need to relax, I tell myself.

On the bus to Dubrovnik, I strike up a conversation in Russian with a woman of thirty from St. Petersburg, travelling with her mother.

"I live in Paris, but now I'm showing Mom around Europe." Russians often speak of their country—and the British Isles—as separate from the Continent. Many revel in Russia's Eur*asian* status, as one nationalist school of thought stresses, an exceptionalism of sorts. "We're going up the Dalmatian Coast, then across Northern Italy. Through Lyons and other French towns. Finally, the City of Light."

Since they're taking budget transportation, they can't be "New Russians" flaunting their wealth. I prefer people who suffer discomfort to see the world over souvenir racks and bridge-divers. I tell her my itinerary. "My Grand Budapest Tour," I add.

"Oh, yes, I've seen this film. It's very popular in Paris."

An hour and a half later, we come to the Croatian border. Guards in dark blue uniforms take cursory glances at most passports, even those of the Russians. But they single out my U.S. documentation and take it into their corrugated tin hut for further scrutiny. They return it ten minutes later with a faint stamp, and we're on our way.

Soon we reach another border post. Back into Bosnia, thanks to the borders drawn by the Dayton Accords. Here they just wave us through, as they do at a second Bosnia-to-Croatia crossing. The bus winds down hairpin curves, moaning in low gear, until glimpses of the bright blue Adriatic come into view amidst karst cliffs. Finally, we cross a modern suspension bridge, with cables slanting down from towers like the ropes from a mast. Sailboats glide through the waters below, leaving short wakes, while cruise ships nudge their square bows forward. Like minnows and sand sharks from our perspective, two hundred feet above.

At the Dubrovnik station, I say goodbye to my Russian companions and head to an ATM with a college-age American woman. We take turns doing guard duty as the other withdraws cash. I'm hardly the only one antsy about potential theft.

She heads to a hostel on the outskirts; I take a shiny yellow city bus to the center of town.

At a gate in the medieval ramparts, I scamper down steps alongside other tourists, clutching my guitar case. The area between the entrance and the massive main wall forms a chamber where a trio plays jazz on clarinet, standup bass, and guitar. Their basket's full of coins and bills, kunas and Euros. Wonder if I could support my stay by busking. Then I notice the sign at the musicians' feet – with their city license number. The clear glissandos of the clarinet, the bassist's left hand dancing nimbly up and down the neck, the guitarist's complex chords. And yet they make it look so easy. Very professional, they must have auditioned for that permit. If I try to play in the center of town, I'll probably get more fines than tips.

Inside the medieval walls, the sun glistens off large white pavement slabs worn smooth by the centuries. One might think it's marble, it's so shiny, but alas, it's only limestone. The renaissance buildings are mostly made of the same material. Male tourists wear bright polo shirts, khaki shorts, leather link belts, and Docksiders. Women are in loose dresses, often covering bathing suits, and straw sun hats with bright bands. College students in tees are the exception. Benetton and other high-end stores occupy the ground floors of historical buildings. How is it I'm getting a room—well, a bed—for twenty-five bucks a night?

I reach my address, press the button. A young female asks my name over the intercom. Within minutes, a rosy-cheeked, sandy-haired fifteen-year-old opens the door. We take two bends in the staircase and reach a landing. Whew! I set my things down.

She winces. "Sorry, we're on the fourth floor."

Golly, that much more to go?

The stairs wrap around three sides of the building for each story inside this tower. By the time we reach reception, I'm covered in perspiration, and my quads ache just above the knees. If Sunday's mountain hike in Bosnia was a half-marathon, this climb has been a demanding sprint. And at check-in I learn my room is yet one floor higher.

It's an eight-bed sleeping quarter, almost as tight as the inside of a submarine. I squeeze my guitar under the bunk and stuff my main bag into a locker. The Euro-style wall AC unit does little to alleviate the humidity from the shower. And I'm going to add more steam, since it will feel like heaven to rinse off a layer of sweat. It's a mixed-gender room, but I take advantage of the fact that no one else is here now and strip down. The stall is narrower than a phone booth, and I bang an elbow turning around in it.

As I dry off, I hear live music: violin, guitar, bass. People are singing along. Kind of like the Gypsy bands I used to hang out with in Slovakia. Maybe I'll get to join in on some songs. Are they in a restaurant in an adjoining building?

At eight-thirty, even though it's still broad daylight two weeks after the solstice, the lights are on in all the brass and iron lanterns over the outdoor tables in every tavern. They seem to be as natural a part of the stone walls as the ubiquitous ivy. Every side street is a staircase leading to more pedestrian thoroughfares near the outer walls. Like having Rome's Spanish Steps on every block.

I ask around about the musicians, hoping I can dine where they're playing. Getting only shrugs, I give up and slump into a chair at one of the ubiquitous outdoor tables. Soon I'm slurping sparkling Italian Acqua Panna from a liter bottle and sipping a glass of crisp, fruity local Chenin Blanc. The sea trout, from Dubrovnik's market, is nothing special – I'm not a huge seafood fan, despite having grown up near the Chesapeake Bay. But I'm famished.

Back in my room, I find an old woman rearranging clothes in her luggage. Her name is Anneke. "I'm traveling all over Europe," she says. "I grew up in the Netherlands but spent most of my life in Canada. Haven't been back to the Old Country much." She breathes heavily. Even in the dim light varicose veins show near her ankles. She has deep wrinkles but her hair, slightly curly, is more black than gray. "Just visited my Dutch relatives. They tried to talk me out of the rest of this trip. 'No, you should just stay here with us. Don't go to the Balkans at your age,' they said. But I'm incorrigible."

I tell her about my trip as I crawl under the covers and switch off the reading light over my bed. I'm starting to feel a bit comfortable here. Like a member of the brotherhood of travelers. And the quarters are probably no more cramped than most medieval pilgrims would have dealt with.

She says, "I'm going down the coast to Greece on the way to Turkey. Anyway, how'd you like Sarajevo?"

I recall my experiences, concluding that it really felt safe.

"I just might make the detour," she says.

I fall asleep in the silence. During the night I rouse a couple of times as younger hostellers return from bar hopping. But only momentarily. My fatigue deadens all but dreams – of minarets, and wars, and the crystalline Adriatic.

* * *

I wake up a full nine hours later.

Anneke is zipping up a valise. "I've slept on what you told me about Sarajevo, and I've decided to go."

I'm startled she's decided so quickly. And on my advice?

She hastens to reassure me. "Don't worry. I'm used to takin' my chances. My family thinks I'm crazy. Eighty years old and travelin' alone, ya know?"

Whoa. I hope I'm still touring the world at her age.

"Besides, I don't care anymore." She smiles. "If I die on this trip, it's better than goin' out in an old folks' home in Canada, no?"

I give her the thumbs up and wish her a safe journey as she rolls her luggage out the door.

With the room empty, I rearrange my clothes, papers, and electronics. I dig in my backpack for sheet music, since I hope to sing a couple of songs with the group I heard last night. Nothing there. I spread everything out on the bed. Still no luck. I run down to the reception to use the wifi, and email Neno, my host in Sarajevo, to see if he's seen the folder with my song collection. This could be a disastrous loss. After fretting over it for a few more minutes, I pack everything up and head outside to enjoy what I can.

In the bright morning, just outside the city walls, I find a guided tour. Soon a van is whisking me and a well-tanned middle-aged American couple up to a cliff overlooking the town.

"We're here on a cruise," says the lady, thin gold bracelets jingling as she runs her fingers through blond tresses. "Just have a few hours. Can you recommend any places to go shopping?" she asks the driver.

While he fills her in, I mull over the town's history, what the guide has just recited along with various materials I read before the trip. Dubrovnik. Ragusa in Italian, also in Franz Ferdinand's native German. Long a colony of the Venetian Republic. Ah, those Venetians. Seafaring merchants who had "colonies" this far away. Filthy rich – even today they have the highest incomes in the EU. No surprise they'd have built a prominent city like this. It had its Ottoman period, and of course its Habsburg era. But how did the local Croatian population fare in all this? Not too well under the early Venetians, probably, who ran a slave trade in the eighth century. Until then the Latin word for slave had been *servus*. But when the Venetians started selling Slavs as human property, it became *sclavus*, a Latinized variant of 'Slav.'

The promontory's craggy karst with tall grass and little else remind me of Dame Rebecca West's encyclopedic account of her travels in the Balkans, *Black Lamb and Grey Falcon*. The Venetians, in their lust for timber to build their city, deforested the Adriatic coast so fully that little grows there any more. Venetians 2: Slavs 0.

As I look down on the famed port, both through a telescope and with naked eye, I hear my van mates express anxiousness to get back into town for shopping. I'm much more appreciative of adventurous sorts like Anneke.

Our driver takes us back down to sea level to the skeletal remains of a water purification plant. Not the typical tourist agenda. It's really an old wound the Croats like to show off, even well after the Dayton Accords brought formal reconciliation.

"During the wars of 1990s, Serbs besieged Dubrovnik," our guide says. "Tried to deprive our city of water, and bombed this plant, a human rights violation." A legitimate beef. Yet now, with the horrors of war over, a crystal-clear stream churns among undergrowth and over rocks, to the counterpoint of birds chirping in the trees.

Back in the hostel, I go to the reception area, where backpackers tap at their laptops on a central table, or recline on couches, texting.

I set up my tablet, upload photos to my website, and plan the rest of my day. Then I get Neno's reply: *I asked you when we left the cottage do you got everything. Sorry, but you forgot your music. Want me mail it to you?*

By the time it reaches here, who knows where I'll be. And I'm not sticking around. *Don't bother. Thanks for looking*, I answer. I've got copies of all my songs back home, and enough stored on my tablet and in my head to get by on this trip. A slight setback, but nothing disastrous.

I try to get a nice lunch by the harbor, but every time I try to browse the menus in the restaurant marquis, a hostess pops out from her station and asks, "Would you like to have lunch with us?" Polite and yet obtrusive.

"No thanks." I move on, not bothering to disguise my annoyance at the pushiness. I fill a plastic liter bottle from a public fountain on the side of a building. Oh, how pure the water is here. And free.

I've dreamed of seeing Dubrovnik for years. I'm glad to have seen the stunning fortifications, their circular corner ramparts like muscular shoulders. Like bunkers, only tempered by good architectural taste. Still, with the crude commercialism, and the overcrowded hostel full of sexual tension—but, I'm guessing, not much actual release—I suddenly want to be done with Dubrovnik.

I grab a quick bite at a gyro stand outside the old city walls and plot my next move.

In the evening, I alight at a restaurant owned by a Russian woman and find the ensemble I heard last night. They wear black slacks, white linen shirts with billowy sleeves, and red sashes around their waists, ends hanging to their knees. Like pirates – or Gypsies. I ask the owner to join me and the musicians on "Moscow Nights." I use her as a prompt for the Russian lyrics left in my folder in Sarajevo. The violin is sweet, the bassline improvised but flawless. The guitarist fills in with delicate finger work. As we finish, he seems eager to play more with us, but the other two want to move on.

Hoping they'll be back, I ask the waiter for paper and jot down the words to "Those Were the Days" as best I can from memory. I hope I can get some video, but I can only find the two-meg card for my digital camera. What happened to the sixteen-meg I've been using? Don't tell me that's back in Sarajevo, too.

I excuse myself to the server and run around the corner and up the five flights to my room. Growing nervous and sweaty, I ransack my belongings in the crowded dorm – no luck. The two-meg card will have to do.

Back at the restaurant, I order wine and fresh, grilled tuna. But I feel distraught over the whole affair of my misplaced items. I finish as twilight comes on. To distract myself, I chat with a couple from the next table, Australians here for a wedding.

Then I spy the guitarist lumbering down the street, absent the other members of his group. He approaches me, smiles, tells me his name is Zoran. "I'm sorry, the other guys go home. But still... You want to do another song now?"

"Well, sure." I hum a bit of "Those Were the Days." Anxious for video material, I hand my cam to the Aussie guy, who obliges.

The guitarist takes a seat at my table and strums E minor.

I stand and sing from the scrawled cue card in my palm. "Once upon a time there was a tavern."

Zoran changes chords and I follow, gaining confidence: "Where we used to raise a glass or two."

Back to E minor: "Remember how we laughed away the hours..."

Then a lingering seventh chord: "... and dreamed of all the great things we would do..." We dive into the refrain, looking each other in the eye to make sure we're in sync on the variable rhythm. "Thooooose weeeeeere the days my friend, we thought they'd never end, we'd sing and dance forever and a day."

Suddenly everyone on the street is clapping along. A twenty-something, who's been snapping shots of his girlfriend on the steps nearby, turns and joins in. Diners at tables in neighboring restaurants also pick up the tune. I'm filled with nervous excitement at being the master of it all. I sing a verse of the original Russian. Blue-eyed Zoran may not be a Roma, but this tune certainly has that Gypsy appeal. We wind down to cheers.

My Australian photographer hands my digital back to me. "Sorry, mate, but it cut off halfway through. Out of memory."

I replay it – at least the first verse is all there. A Russian girl of ten approaches shyly from the next outdoor restaurant and hands me a ten-kuna tip. So I earned money on the streets of Dubrovnik! More importantly, I'm touched by the gesture, so I chat briefly with her parents.

Back at my table, Zoran asks, "Will you be here tomorrow?" My "no" evokes a pained look.

"I'm really sorry, I have to get back to Prague before long. Then America." We exchange cards. "I really hope we can make music together again."

Now it seems a pity to leave, but this town's too expensive, too crowded. Too many more places to see. Trieste, Vienna. And maybe it's best to leave on a high note.

* * *

From the roadway a hundred feet above the Adriatic, the bus offers views of clear waters, cruise ships, sailboats, and commercial fishing vessels. Green isles with white beaches spread out lazily offshore. Italian-style bell towers peek out from among cypresses and palms growing up from the hills, which slope toward the sand below.

I've been looking forward to my next destination, the resort of Split (pronounced spleet), since my grad school days, when I read in a Serbo-Croatian textbook about its founding as a Greek colony and its later role as Diocletian's resort and retirement home. This man of humble background was born in the area and rose through the military to become Roman emperor. In 303-311, he conducted persecutions even more ferocious than those of Nero, but to no avail – Christianity became a state religion (one of several officially tolerated, not the only one, as is often misstated) under Constantine in 324. This coastal region, Dalmatia, got its name from the language of the Illyrians, a people of antiquity whose origins are still hotly debated among scholars. South Slavs yearning to unite in the 1800s cited them as common ancestors, although there actually was no appreciable Slavic presence here until the seventh century AD, when Slav tribes began raiding parties against the Balkans' Latin and Greek populations. Like the larger Pan-Slavism, Illyrianism looked back on an illusory golden age.

Along the highway, bumblebee-yellow signs announce the names of towns in black Latin script with smaller Cyrillic lettering below for Croatia's remaining Serbs, those not ethnically cleansed two decades ago. Often, the minority language is slashed through with spray paint.

But my gaze is fixed largely to my left, to the west, where islands of various shapes and sizes lace the coastline. The Archduke would have seen them, I recall, from the other side – aboard the Viribus Unitis on the Adriatic.

Upon my arrival at the station, right next to a busy wharf, thirty-year-old hostel owner Mirjana picks me up in her 1990s compact. My stuff barely fits, but, hey, I've never had a courtesy shuttle with this sort of accommodation. I'm in a discount Riviera.

"Good thing you made it when you did." She puffs, flipping a dark curl from her eyes. "I'll be busy with check-ins later. I might even sell out tonight."

She lets me out in front of a four-story building. Horizontal grooves a foot apart run the length of the robin-egg stucco exterior. The bulky ten-foot wooden door opens to a nine-teenth-century stage-coach entrance and a huge staircase to the second story. I trudge up to a reception area where a World Cup match blares from a large-screen TV. The place has a modern kitchenette and small, shared baths/showers for each sex. Each bedroom has a theme color: plum, orange, lime. Seems I left mauve and beige behind in Bosnia and Herzegovina. A mop and bucket stand in the corner. Four-foot square windows have been swiveled open to allow bleach fumes to dissipate.

After checking me in, Mirjana recommends a restaurant three blocks off, tucked away, oddly, between a tin-roofed Quonset hut and a nineteenth-century brick building. Not much air stirs in the courtyard, and I think for a moment of going elsewhere. But the six tables of diners chatting under two large oaks seem inviting. So I order mussels on a bed of extra-wide spinach fettucine. The dish's tomato sauce is thinned by the broth that cooks off from the shellfish. A mug of Karlovačko, a Croatian pale lager with a good head and hint of bitterness, rounds out the meal.

After dark, I saunter down to the quay, where tables with starched linens echo with the chitchat of wealthy clientele. On the other side of the pedestrian boulevard, waves lap against a retaining wall. A group of young British bar hoppers stumbles along, arm-in-arm. Closer to the shore, couples talk and smooch on benches under the palms.

* * *

The following noon, I catch a reenactment of Roman pageantry. Soldiers in brush-topped helmets, crimson tunics, and bronze armor line the colonnade on the approach to the peristyle. Some stand with spears firmly planted on the stone steps. Others beat drums to announce the imperial couple's arrival on the portico. The toga-clad actors mimicking Diocletian and his wife wave to the crowds in straw hats, baseball caps, and sunglasses, who snap pictures as frenetically as if modern-day world leaders had appeared.

The spectacle is over in minutes, and everyone resumes sightseeing. It's the world's largest and most complete remains of a Roman palace, a complex within a several-acre square in Split's center. My tabloid-sized foldout map in shades of tan shows forty historical sites from gates to fountains to churches.

I visit Diocletian's Mausoleum and a church where John Paul II celebrated Mass on several visits. Near the outer walls of the center, the Ethnographic Museum displays costumes of various regions from the coastal south to the mountainous interior which borders on Hungary to the north and Serbia to the east. The whole country looks like a scythe blade curling around Bosnia. Nationalist Croats still talk about carving out a chunk of B and H to fill in the middle.

With Roman rituals crossed off my list, I pick up bread, salami, and veggies – and an extra sixteen-gig memory card for more pics and video. My room is empty now, between check-in and check-out times, so I spread out my belongings on my bed. The large-capacity card I was afraid I'd lost, the once I should have used for my impromptu performance in Dubrovnik, falls out of a rolled-up tee shirt. I just need time, space, and privacy to get things reorganized.

Mirjana—who performs every job from maid to receptionist to concierge—isn't too busy at lunchtime, so I ask about transport to Rijeka. I'd like to take a boat, to say that I've cruised up the Adriatic, to round out my trip by plane, train, car, bus, and van. And to better retrace Franz Ferdinand's travels. But the only routes available are overnight, and I'd be sleeping on deck in heaven knows what weather.

"Where would I stow my luggage?" I ask our hostel owner.

"I'm afraid I can't tell you about that. You'd have to call the shipping line."

Okay, she bends over backwards, as budget accommodations go. I can't expect her to play travel agent, too. I'd like to get up to Rijeka soon, then go west to Trieste, Italy before hitting Slovenia, which I've only managed to travel through thus far. Daunted over the uncertainties, I consider a train trip to Zagreb, although it'll be a repeat visit for me.

* * *

I sleep extraordinarily well at night, since Mirjana cranked up the flat AC unit in the hall before crashing on the reception couch. She sold out the house. I'm glad for her.

But I awake at five to warm humidity. Though Mirjana had gotten everyone to agree to leave the bedroom doors open to let the cool air in, someone has closed ours. I suspect it's the Bolivians in the top bunks. By the light of my cell phone, I can see them wrapped up in the blankets that all the other residents have tossed aside. Different culture, different attitude. East Europeans are afraid of catching their death from icy drinks, while Mexicans find them soothing for a sore throat. There are bound to be conflicts over night air. So I'm not angry at the South Americans, just irritated at the circumstances. I crawl from bed and open the door. But even at seven, the cool air isn't filling the room back up. I try taking a walk around the block, but it only leaves me with a wide-awake-but-not-well-rested feeling. To make things worse, my lower back is starting to tighten up. Maybe the cool morning air wasn't such a great idea.

Back at the hostel, I beg Mirjana, "Please tell me you're not sold out tonight."

"Don't worry, I've got beds left." She purses her lips, then puffs a cigarette.

"I have another problem. My back is getting really stiff. Where could I get a massage?"

"I can have a masseuse come here." She puts her Marlboro out, and within thirty seconds, she's speaking Croatian on her iPhone.

By noon, most guests have checked out, leaving me the six-bed room to myself. A petite blonde in bright-green tee and sweat pants lumbers up the large staircase, carrying a fold-up massage table with the help of an assistant. A couple of American guys having lunch in the kitchenette gawk and joke about what kind of massage I'm getting.

"C'mon now, they're good girls," Mirjana insists with a bemused smile.

"No happy end," I say, getting a few chuckles from the crowd.

Soon the blonde's small but powerful fingers are running up and down the tiny muscles that attach to my spine, loosening the bruisy-feeling knots. Knowing I speak Slovak, she switches to Croatian when her English doesn't suffice. Her voice is soothing, full of sympathy. I catch a Slavic word for "fluids"—probably a reference to lymphatic drainage—as she makes a smooth gentle motion just below my shoulder blade, where minutes before she'd been kneading deeply. I drift into a pampered drowse. After an hour, she has me stand, slowly, as I'm so relaxed I could crumple to the floor. I pay the equivalent of forty bucks in local kunas and thank her profusely in English, Slovak, and broken Croat.

"You should drink much water. To rinse out toxins," she says as she leaves.

I crawl back into bed and nap as, just outside the window blinds, motor scooters and economy cars buzz by. It's time to slow down. At forty-eight, I don't fit in with this young crowd. But I can't afford luxury hotels every night. And I enjoy seeing the success of an entrepreneur like Mirjana.

I should have gotten in better shape before coming here. Not that I lead a terribly sedentary lifestyle, but touring without a car requires stamina. Hmm, wonder how eighty-year-old Anneke is doing. Probably seen Sarajevo by now and headed back down the Adriatic towards Greece. I take courage from her example.

In the afternoon, I take a casual stroll through a residential section of the old quarter where vines with copious magenta buds cover the off-white wall on one side of a building. The terracotta roof and green shutters complete the harmony of Mediterranean color and style. The architecture reminds me so much of Italy, but everyone speaks a Slavic language. Then I go lie in the grass of a small park and listen to birds in the shade trees overhead.

Hearing bells nearby just before five, I decide to attend Mass. I wouldn't normally choose a twentieth-century building – this thing is awfully blocky, a piece of "functionalism" from the 1920s. But it's actually a Franciscan church called "Our Lady of Health." Maybe I should pray to her to cure my back.

I'm drawn to a fresco of Saints Cyril and Methodius, the "Apostles to the Slavs," on the back wall of a side chapel. A Slavic-Greek bilingual from Thessalonica, Cyril created a written language for the Slavs in the ninth century. Behind them, spread across a map of the Adriatic Coast, people a tenth their size stand in folk costumes from more recent centuries. An unconventional representation of the heritage the two Thessalonian brothers bequeathed to Croatians. They hold a paper with geometric figures: an hourglass, two triangles point-to-point, an irregular quadrangle with a T in the middle, the letter E turned on its back. The Glagolitic alphabet – the one that Cyril invented. (I recognize it from a grad school course in medieval Slavic manuscripts; it was his disciples, most scholars agree, who invented the Cyrillic script named for him.) The brothers are painted in a modern style as close to Fauvism (like Matisse) as anything, with a bit of cubism playing on the blocky Glagolitic characters. While the brothers' mission was to Great Moravia, a territory that lay in today's Czech Republic and Slovakia, the Glagolitic tradition spread to the Dalmatian isles and is still maintained in monasteries there. I'd like to visit them someday, but it'll have to wait for another trip.

Cyril and Methodius are revered by both Catholic and Orthodox Christians for their quintessential role in Slavic Christian culture. During the Mass, I receive communion, return to my pew and kneel, and pray that Serbs, Croats, and others will find ways to celebrate this common heritage rather than fight over it.

With this sentiment in mind, I go to the station and buy a ticket for the morning train to Zagreb. This will be an inland detour from Franz Ferdinand's Adriatic tour by warship, but it's an important locale of the old Empire.

9

Under Strossmayer's Watchful Gaze in Zagreb

On the ride from the Adriatic Coast to the interior, the locomotive chugs up arid hills with sparse shrubbery and even fewer trees. Now I'm convinced of Dame Rebecca West's claim in *Black Lamb and Grey Falcon* that Venetians, greedy for timber pilings upon which to expand their merchant city, deforested much of the Balkans centuries ago. I start to nod off but the diesel engine, straining with the climb, makes my seat shudder. When I lean into the space between headrest and window, the thick glass pane rattles my skull.

We coast downhill more frequently in the central valleys, but still only average about forty miles per hour, much like the train I took from Budapest to the south of Hungary two and a half weeks ago. There are few villages along the route, and one medium-sized town. Only a half-dozen stops on a five-hour trip, which justifies calling it an "express."

Streams trickle and meander through the dales, giving rise to green patches of marsh grass and willows. Whitewashed cottages speckle the landscape. Finally, six hours into the journey, we enter suburbs where rustbelt mingles with garish billboards. White-and-gray Tito-era prefab housing projects jut their monotones into the sky, but some are being brightened up in fresh pastel paint, like a black-and-white movie that suddenly switches to color.

Ambling out Zagreb's station hall into late-afternoon sunlight, I'm greeted by a bronze equestrian statue of Tomislav, Croatia's first king in the tenth century, atop a red marble plinth. He's surrounded by a grassy square and wide boulevards, an oddly open space for a capital city's center. Some hundred yards away four-story nineteenth-century buildings rise. The copper domes on their corners remind me of Budapest – even of some buildings in Banská Bystrica, a provincial Slovak town I lived in for three years. With their smooth masonry—even if their coats of paint are chipped and sooty—they feel less Mediterranean and more Central European, not like the Italian-style rough-hewn stone buildings in Split and Dubrovnik.

The last time I was here, I arrived on a bus with a Slovak choir from Banská Bystrica, after the first part of our circuit through northern Italy. This time, I get to explore the city on foot for three days, rather than zipping from site to site in a single afternoon, and in a crowded coach, at that. Back then my Slovak colleagues and our Croatian hosts spoke of centuries of Hungarian oppression with nodding all around. As fellow Slavs they had a common gripe. Tomislav's realms eventually came under the sway of Hungarian kings. Even then the Croats maintained their own principalities with special privileges. Medieval Slovak cities also had more autonomy than nationalist narratives let on. Banská Bystrica's government used German and Slovak as official languages for some time during the Renaissance – the Germans had settled there as tradespeople. It was only in the 1820s that Budapest began curtailing linguistic rights of Slavic nationalities. In the 1860s, things got nastier with the closing of Slovak schools, which threatened to erode national literacy, for all but those who adopted the Magyar tongue, becoming "Magyarones," or Hungarian wannabes.

My hostel is just three blocks from the station, a three-story dorm with college kids milling about the lobby and older folks behind the reception desk. Eager for more privacy—and sleep—I get a room all to myself. Two beds: I lay my guitar and spread out clothes for sorting on one. Then open the large swivel window and ease my tired frame onto the other.

I'm stiff again, as if the vibrating train has given me a reverse massage, undoing all the good from yesterday's backrub in Split. I should've walked the aisle to stay limber. I lie down, stretch to loosen my lower back, take a nap, and then I'm ready to explore the town.

Well behind King Tomislav stands the yellow Art Pavilion. The taller, central part of its roof is made of glass rectangles and triangles, a bit like the dome of Berlin's Bundestag, glistening silvery in the sun like fish scales.

Behind the Pavilion is another football-field-sized lawn. On this summer day, it's full of food carts and booths displaying crafts and souvenirs, many draped with twinkling strings of tiny white lights. Folks recline on wooden folding chairs here, plastic patio chairs there, at tables with umbrellas advertising Karlovačko beer, with the same red-and-white checkered pattern as that on the label – or in the Croatian coat of arms. Charcoal and cigarette smoke waft among people in their twenties and thirties to the din of sizzling sausages and chatter.

At the head of the U-shaped arrangement of stalls, at the foot of a statue, four guys twist forearms like mad at a foosball table. Around it sprawl armchairs in faded tangerine, mauve, and Granny-Smith apple. Late sixties stuff, possibly early seventies – just like the Grand Budapest Hotel's lobby during its socialist period. It reminds me of my earliest days in Slovakia, just after the communist collapse. Ah, those were the days: conversations about the country's future, and the meaning of Václav Havel's plays, shoulder-to-shoulder with teaching colleagues around low cocktail tables in the much less grand Hotel Turiec in Martin, Slovakia.

I grab a sour-cherry schnapps from a booth offering plum, pear, apricot, and other fruit distillations and think back to the pálinka-menu in Villány, Hungary, my friend's homemade stuff in Martin, and the rakija Neno gave me in Sarajevo. Man, these Central Europeans can make a grappa out of anything.

A stage is set with stands, mikes, and amps, but recorded music plays from the speakers. A couple of guys stand on the pavement around it, setting their bottles of Karlovačko on the edge of the platform at belly-button level.

"Are you in charge here?" I ask a carrot-topped guy in his mid-twenties, as his buddy slips off to chat with some girls at a table.

"I'm one of the organizers. Why?"

"Do you have some kind of open mike?"

"Huh?" He wrinkles reddish brows. His English is quite good, but it doesn't seem to include obscure American slang.

"I mean, when amateur musicians can play a few songs."

"Yeah, we might do something like that tomorrow. Come back in early afternoon and ask."

Oh yes, that Slavic aversion to overscheduling. I remember it well.

We introduce ourselves—he's Juraj, or "George"—and he explains that the event is a decentralized, more-or-less spontaneous youth festival.

The statue, I now notice, is a robed priest seated on a plinth behind the stage, like a larger-than-life drummer at the back of the band. Probably the archbishop's statue mentioned in *Black Lamb and Grey Falcon*.

"Is that Strossmayer?" I ask.

"Yeah. He donated about half the artwork in the museum behind us." Juraj, beaming, motions toward a cream-colored building.

"Yeah, I read about how much he did for the Croats, even though he was an Austrian."

"Exactly." He nods.

"It was in a book by Rebecca West. I assume you've heard of her."

"Sure. I haven't read much of it, but I thought she favored the Serbs."

To avoid ethnic disputes, I steer away from the Croats-versus-Serbs discussion. "I thought she was more anti-Habsburg than anything. Whenever Franz Joseph did anything good, she had to find an ulterior motive. If he gave one ethnic group in the empire a privilege, it was to evoke the jealousy of another. Divide and conquer."

"There's some truth to that. Still, we Croats aren't all that anti-Habsburg. After all, they're Catholic like us."

"And Strossmayer." Presumably he's not too controversial.

"Yeah, he was much less authoritarian than the emperor."

The bronze archbishop has a hand on one knee, the other outstretched. The long, tapered fingers suggest he would have made a good guitarist. Clearly was interested in the arts, a major patron, probably was musically inclined. His head is tilted; a serene smile curves his lips. I fancy he enjoys quietly presiding over this youth scene, a ghostly chaperone from the past. The partying crowd, friendly but not rowdy, doesn't mind—or doesn't notice?—his benevolent oversight.

* * *

In the morning I peruse Strossmayer's collections in the Gallery of Old Masters, just behind the statue of the archbishop, who established the building to house the Academy of Arts and Sciences. It holds works by Venetian and Florentine masters from various schools of the fourteenth to the nineteenth centuries. Out back stands a knee-high, eight-foot wide, granite replica of an engraving with more of those triangles, circles, arcs: the now-familiar Glagolitic alphabet of Saint Cyril. I run my hands over the chiseled letters, fingertips sinking into the grooves. A caption says the original of the document is kept in Rijeka, the next stop on my revised itinerary. So, although I won't have time for the coastal-island Dalmatian monasteries with their centuries-old Glagolitic tradition, I may still get to see a manuscript in this alphabet.

It's sunny but breezy, taking me back to that June of 1995 when our busload of Slovak choristers disembarked from our stuffy tin can into the fresh air outside Zagreb's Mirogoj Cemetery. Copious dark-green ivy crawled the white walls like a joyous throng of M.C. Escher salamanders, lending vitality to the remembrance of the dead. Inside the complex lay hundreds of graves among the porticos. Most of the fresh-cut flowers went to the heroes of the Slavic world: poets, historians, and linguists as much as generals or politicians. The Slovaks I was traveling with back then required little introduction, as schoolbooks had made sure they knew the main figures of the Illyrian movement, the South Slavic branch of pan-Slavism. We paused at the grave of Ljudevit Gaj, I recall. Although a native German-speaker with French Huguenot origins, whose family came from today's Slovakia, he codified a grammar of Croatian, and obtained permission from Vienna to publish a newspaper in that language. Croats greatly esteemed his legacy, judging by the five floral arrangements that stood in front of his tombstone.

Returning to the present, I stumble upon a downtown gallery with a sandwich board advertising a concert, part of the Zagreb Summer Nights series. A college student with a temporary docent job shows me the program of "Young Croatian Stars," featuring an up-and-coming pianist named Aljoša Jurinić and the Croatian String Quartet. Given the dozens of locals waiting at the museum ticket counter, I figure I've lucked out for Monday entertainment.

"We've only got a few tickets left," says the twenty-something docent.

But the gathering audience peers anxiously at the sky, where the sultry afternoon air has given birth to menacing dark clouds, their edges like halos of sunlight.

"What if it rains?"

"Don't worry, we'll refund."

Two minutes after I buy my ticket, rain patters in the courtyard. The docent pulls up a radar map on her smartphone. We're on the southern edge of a system moving northeastward. Ten minutes later, the sky is clear. Employees hurriedly wipe off the plastic café chairs and usher the audience out into their seats, while five guys roll a black Steinway from its haven under the eaves onto center stage. For the sake of the instrument, I hope it doesn't start showering again, even if they do have a tarp to protect it.

But the air is now cool and dry, as the three-story building shades us from the early-July sun. A twenty-something Aljoša Jurinić, who the program promises is "one of the most talented young Croatian pianists," takes his bow and lights into the *Allegro assai* opening of Schubert's *Drei Klavierstücke*. After the three movements of that piece, the quartet comes onstage for two short works by Croatian composer Blagoje Bersa, about whom I know nothing. His "Melancholy" contains doleful but seductive Gypsy-like lines, but "On the Beach" is a peppy Slavic folk tune. After a brief intermission, the pianist returns for two Liszt pieces. The finale is his Hungarian Rhapsody no. 11. I've heard the famous no. 2 a gazillion times, but this is a delightful change of pace. The five-minute composition rushes from the opening arpeggios into breakneck hammering in a passable imitation of the Hungarian dulcimer. The artist must be a virtuoso to handle these and other of Liszt's notoriously difficult techniques.

The mostly Croatian crowd cheers and rises to applaud as the final chords die out. I stand, comforted that *these* Zagrebers, unlike nationalists in the region, embrace the Hungarian elements of their Central European heritage. Multi-ethnic consciousness is still alive and kicking, at least in some places.

Back in my dorm room, I swing the window open, letting in balmy night air. A lone violin warbles from one of the apartments across the courtyard from the hostel. The person is probably just practicing, but the tone is rich, not that of an amateur. It's a minor-mode piece I've never heard.

Maybe the violinist is a Roma, I wonder as I drift off to sleep.

* * *

On the way to the "Upper Town" in the morning, I happen upon the city's public transport hub. A blackened bronze equestrian statue towers over the tram stops and bus shelters. Even in that dark metal monotone, a Hussar jacket is recognizable by the horizontal braids connecting the buttonholes on the chest. The figure wears a cap with a single feather in front, more Hungarian influence. He holds a saber forward, his arm arched so that the curved blade seems an extension of his body. It's a memorial to Ban Jelačić. The title ban, probably of Turkic origin, translates roughly as "viceroy." Jelačić held the rank in the mid-nineteenth century, when he helped Austria suppress the Hungarian Revolution of 1848. He curried favor with the Habsburgs in hopes of winning some level of independence for Croatia. Treachery from the Magyars' point of view. He joined Austrians, Croats, Slovaks, and Russians in putting down the Hungarian uprising. Still, he abolished the serfdom within his realms – which the Hungarian Diet had also done. The reforms of the era were all but unstoppable by then. So in some sense, Jelačić was a progressive – for his time. Sort of.

The twin spires of the Cathedral of Sts. Peter and Paul dominate Zagreb's skyline, so the scaffolding covering one of them catches my eye. A photograph of the obscured section of the building, printed on a cloth the length of three bedspreads, hangs from the structure. It's a bit windy on the square in front, where the Virgin atop a thirty-foot column seems to emit rays of light: the sun reflecting from her golden coating.

Inside, it's cooler. I've come to revisit the Glagolitic inscription on a wall at the end of a side aisle. The circles, polygons, and squiggles of this mysterious script are about a foot tall, with sixteen lines of verse, all above statues of Christ and the two thieves crucified with him.

Back near the entrance I find the graves of two Croats executed in 1671 for leading a revolt against Habsburg rule. Petar Zrinski and Fran Krsto Frankopan were buried inside a marble wall here after their bones were moved from Wiener Neustadt, near Vienna, in 1919. Neither the Zrinyis, some of whom were Bans of Croatia, nor the Frankopans, a noble clan said to be related to the Italian Frangipani, considered themselves as members solely of one nation or another, either Croat or Magyar.

I feel a literary connection to Petar's brother Miklós Zrinyi, as he's known in Hungarian, having read his book-length verse *The Siege of Sziget*, about his eponymous great-grandfather's exploits in the Hungarian-Turkish wars of the sixteenth century. Miklós Zrinyi wrote in Hungarian, although he was equally proficient in Croatian. (Fortunately, this important work was translated, in full, into English a few years ago, but there are still some essential works of Hungarian literature that have not been translated.) Petar's wife, Ana Katarina, Fran Krsto Frankopan's half-sister, also contributed significantly to the development of Magyar letters. The Zrinskis' and Frankopans' loyalty to the historical multi-ethnic Hungary is emblematic of a time well before the modern nation-state. But their rebellion, some say, stemmed from dissatisfaction that the Austrians had failed to expel the Turks from *all* of the Kingdom of Hungary – at a time when Hungary was just emerging from 150 years of Ottoman conquest and rule. They were executed in Wiener Neustadt for this "Magnate Conspiracy."

It's curious how towns in the old empire honor both Habsburg enemies and allies. Ah, the cognitive dissonance of history.

Behind the main altar is a figure of modern Croat history. Cardinal Alojs Stepinac's embalmed body lies in a glass coffin, in bishop's miter and red vestments, which oddly reminds me of Lenin's tomb in Moscow – without the waiting line. His skin looks like plaster—or something out of Madame Tussaud's—but it is his actual body. More controversial is his cooperation with the fascist Ustaše regime installed in Croatia after Hitler invaded to "save" the country from Serbian oppression. Yet, while Stepinac appeared numerous times at official Ustaše events, he eventually came to be horrified at atrocities against Jews. Behind the scenes, he lent aid to them and to Serbs escaping persecution. He did state publicly that they were fellow humans who deserved to be treated with dignity, and wrote private letters urging the government to exercise moderation, but shied from criticizing the regime openly. After the war, Tito's communist government convicted him of treason, yet many insist the documents used against him were forged. He died in 1960, after serving a five-year sentence, then being placed under house arrest following a diagnosis of a rare blood disease. Some say the secret police poisoned him, then removed his heart and (possibly) other organs after his death, and burned them to destroy the evidence.

At any rate, he was exhumed and put here, in the seat of the primate, in 1993. Five years later, Pope John Paul II beatified him as a martyr for his anti-communism, in particular for resisting Tito's efforts to sever, or at least weaken, ties between the Croatian Catholic Church and Rome. East-European leaders typically dreaded "Vatican spies" – or any supranational allegiance that might challenge Party rule. And though Stepinac empathized with non-Catholics during the war, in the years that followed he seems to have feared communism more than he ever did fascism. If so, I think it was because fascism may have compromised the Church, and sent priests—especially Polish ones—to the concentration camps, but communists threatened the Church's very existence.

Back outdoors, I get lost on a street of artisans' booths selling to tourists. I turn around and aim for what I think is a street named for the very uncontroversial Archbishop Strossmayer, only to find I'm on something called the *Ilica*. I realize that my pocket map shows no topography, and my destination is up a very steep hill. After a moment's frustration, I'm relieved to find that there's a funicular up to the *Gorni grad* or "Upper Town." A way of reaching my destination without the climb. Inside the miniscule station, I spot a ticket booth and pull out a five-kuna banknote. On the back are Zrinyi and Frankopan. History lesson consolidated!

I exit the funicular to see a sign announcing Strossmartre, in the Art Nouveau style of the oft-photoed Parisian metro station "Montmartre." It's the *Strossmayerova šetalište*, Strossmayer's promenade. The name reminds me that Hungarian and Croatian share a verb root *setal*, meaning to take a stroll. It's a small park, a path of fine gravel shaded by oaks and linden trees. Couples pushing prams stop to buy ice cream and sodas from pine-plank booths lining the way near the entrance. I cool off on a bench, hoping the benign memories of the good archbishop Strossmayer outshine all the controversial, at times murderous, history of this nation.

Soon I'm wandering the cobblestones of the Upper Town, stopping to gaze at the red-white-and-blue glazed tiles on St. Mark's church. They form coats of arms of Zagreb, Croatia, Slavonia, and Dalmatia, against a checked background. But they lack the luminescence of the eosin glazing of the Hungarian Zsolnays from Pécs. These duller-finished tiles came from the town of Karlovac (like the ubiquitous Karlovačko beer). The use of Croatian national symbols, a bit defiant towards Austro-Hungarian centralism in the 1880s when the church got this renovated roof, was encouraged by none other than Strossmayer.

To the right of St. Mark's Square stands the neo-classical Parliament Building, rebuilt in 1908 to accommodate what little autonomy Croatia had. It was from the balcony that total independence from Austria-Hungary was declared in October 1918, before war's end, even before Yugoslavia's creation had become a sure thing.

My feet are so weary, I decide to take the funicular *downhill*. Along Masaryk Street, named for the first post-World War I president of Czechoslovakia, vines and other climbers on apartment balconies give things a distinctly southern European feel. A statue of Serbian inventor Nikola Tesla is a reminder that I'm in the Balkans – and that Croats still honor some of their eastern neighbors. Things open up onto Petar Preradović Square, where bike racks sit under ten-year-old elms in tree cages. Cafés are all around, tables full of coffee and beer drinkers, shaded by canopies advertising Tchibo coffee and Karlovačko beer. Chatter competes with street musicians in front of a statue of Petar Preradović, a nineteenth-century Croatian poet. Although he first wrote in German, he soon developed an interest in cultivating Croatian verse. His poetic stirrings began while at the military academy in Wiener Neustadt. In keeping with the cognitive dissonance of Austro-Hungarian history, he fought against the Italians trying to unify their country and was eventually ennobled and promoted to general, while his granddaughter, Paula von Preradović, went on to write the lyrics of the modern anthem of the Republic of Austria.

The musicians playing at his bronze feet sound like pros. Soprano sax, acoustic guitar and accordion play a tuneful, upbeat version of the otherwise tragic Russian "Dark Eyes." It's not a song for dancing or clapping, but the rapt onlookers applaud heartily at the end, then toss a shower of coins. I chat briefly with the band members, from Bulgaria and Romania, who are on a summer-long Balkan tour.

As much as I'd like to linger, I want to take in more architecture on this, my last day. So I go back out to the large grassy lawns near the train station where I arrived two days before to check out a few items I missed. Consulting a remarkably high-quality, free seventy-five-page, full-color guide book, I learn that much of the "Austro-Hungarian" look comes from architects Ferdinand Fellner and Hermann Helmer. The duo designed theaters all over the Empire: Vienna, Budapest, Bratislava, Karlsbad and Brno in today's Czech Republic, Szeged in Hungary, towns in Transylvania; as well as buildings outside of the Monarchy, like Zurich, Hamburg, Sofia, and Odessa. Here, the Croatian National Theater seems typical of their designs: a ribbed-masonry ground floor supports two stories of columned neo-classical façade. A circle drive allows aristocrats' coaches to pull into a sheltered entrance, staying dry even during the heaviest of rains. Above that structure is a large balcony with two-foot-high concrete railing, much like a portico on a country chateau. The yellow paint with cream trim gives it a stately and serene Germanic look, elegant but not overindulgent. I've suddenly unlocked a huge riddle, why so many towns of Austria-Hungary seemed to have been part of a large, spread-out architectural ensemble. Strange to think that so much of it was the work of just two men.

As dusk falls, I go once more to the youth festival, try a couple of fruity schnapps, apricot and pear this time. Then I get a bottled Karlovačko and settle one last time into a "Grand Budapest" lounge chair. Exhausted from pounding the pavement, I slump lower, look around at the families and young people, and take one more glance at the paternal figure of Strossmayer.

Then I spot the festival organizer I met two nights ago. Juraj, "Carrot-top," in tee-shirt and jeans, is wrapping up a chat with a friend. I approach and greet him, then say, "These are my last few hours here."

"What do you think of Zagreb?"

"It's been a good second visit." I tell him about my trip in ninety-five. "Great to explore more fully on foot now. Lively town." I pause. "I've just been to Sarajevo."

"Oh, really? I was born there. But I'm Croat, you know."

I mention the Muslim character of the Bosnian capital.

He looks a little surprised. "But it isn't – or wasn't. At least not until the Serbs declared their 'Republika Srbska' and made their neighborhoods independent of the city. Christians—Orthodox and Catholic together—were in majority."

I'm disappointed at his obvious resentment – it would be nice to hear more tones of reconciliation in this formerly war-torn area. I'm not even sure if his main beef is with the Serbs or the Bosniaks.

"Anyway, I'm thinking about moving back there," he continues. "Things are getting too expensive here in Zagreb."

"Yeah, that's the way it is in the formerly socialist countries." I look back at the furniture from the 1980s, and he follows my gaze. "Have you seen *Grand Budapest Hotel?*"

He purses his lips. "Yes. Wes Anderson creates that sixties-seventies feel. Comforting, in a way. But it's almost gone here. Nothing lasts forever."

We shake hands and I saunter back to the hostel. Maybe I'm chasing too much after a bygone era. Or two such eras: Habsburg and the post-socialist days of my late twenties.

Back in my room, I swivel open the window. Cool air gushes in. Soon strains of that same violin come wafting in as well. Roma? Perhaps. I'll definitely catch up with Roma musician friends in Prague and relive some old times. Pursuing the past, as always. Anyway, familiar faces will bring me cheer, more than this historical town alone could do.

For now, Rijeka and Trieste, my last two Adriatic stops, beckon. Rijeka, I've found out, has a museum with the Glagolitic manuscript replicated in stone behind Strossmayer's gallery. After that comes Vienna and one or two stops in Slovakia. I just have to see some more old friends there – including, if things work out, a violinist, bandleader, and head of gypsymusic.sk. But the road is taking its toll. I'll have to slow down, and skip Graz, Austria, where Franz Ferdinand was born.

10

Return to Adriatica: Rijeka and Trieste

L ight rain streaks the train windows as we pull away and pass by the river. Warehouses give way to cottages near the verdant banks as Zagreb recedes. Hunger takes over my thoughts. I slide my lunch, from a stand at the station, out of my backpack, careful not to squash it further. It's a slice of mushroom pizza in a thin paper sleeve. Beneath a yellow heart and the name Mlinar—"Miller"—is a single wish: *Dobar tek/ Dober tek/Jó étvágyat/Guten Appetit/Bon appétit.* All in languages of the old monarchy, plus the lingua franca of a century ago, French. I guess they left out English, since its best equivalent is the non-literal "Enjoy your meal."

I'm sitting in a wagon section with fold-down seats, simple wood and metal planks, along the wall. I can spread my things out and prepare a "smaller version of my stuff," as George Carlin called it in a popular routine, to take with me to the Rijeka hostel while checking the rest at the station. A couple in red-and-white windbreakers board at the next stop, leaning their bicycles against the wall in the open space next to the cargo door. Judging from their red-and-white pennants and laminated prayer cards with images of John Paul II and Sister Mary Faustina, they must be Polish. Touring Croatian shrines and pilgrimage sites, no doubt.

Soon they get off, and German-speaking parents with a son and daughter get on. They hang some wet clothes on a rail beneath the window. They get settled and start playing a number game with the seven-year-old boy. I hear dialectal forms of numbers: *tsvontskch* for twenty, *fuenftskch* for fifty. Where have I heard that before? Ah, Switzerland!

"*Kommen Sie aus der Schweiz?*" I ask.

"Ja, aus Zürich. We flew into Venice and we've been travelling the Adriatic. Just came inland for a day. After Rijeka, we're touring the Istrian peninsula, then flying back home."

The family has a quiet lunch, speaking Swiss German among themselves. I diddle around on John Denver's "Annie's Song," remembering the chords better than the lyrics. How I miss that sheet music left behind at the mountain cottage outside Sarajevo!

Soon, the ten-year-old daughter lights into the original High German version of "Mack the Knife." I happen to know the song, so I play the chords and try to follow along: *Mackie Messer, der hat Zähne*.... The family runs out of words after a couple of stanzas, so I throw in what I know. "Oh, the shark has, pretty teeth dear, and he shines them, peeeaaarly whiiiiiite." We all have a good laugh, humming along and stumbling through the English and German lyrics.

Shortly before arrival in Rijeka, the train clatters through thick pine forest—apparently, the medieval Venetians didn't deforest the land too close to home—and as we head downhill the Adriatic comes into view once more.

*   *   *

As I check into the youth hostel, I ask the receptionist if he would call the institute with the Glagolitic manuscripts. When I return from stowing things in my room, he says with a sympathetic frown, "They're closed for the summer for renovations." Funny they never mentioned that on their website. So Rijeka will be more of a way station than anything.

I ride to the "top" of town, to the John Paul II Center. The bus, clean and new, winds up streets that cling to the hillsides with help from retaining walls. Guardrails form diagonal outlines on the streets farther uphill, where townhouses and villas in beige and peach stucco with faded green shutters perch among evergreens. Aluminum poles supporting boxy streetlights on a pedestrian bridge add a touch of socialist-era junkiness; this is what Italy might look like if communists had taken over after World War II.

Rijeka is known as Fiume in Italian. Both mean simply "river." Under nineteenth-century Hungarian administration, the city became a magnet for nationalities from around the Empire. Over sixty percent of the population was Italian at the end of the Great War. After agonized international debate—and a stint as the Free State of Fiume, recognized by the League of Nations—Italy annexed it in 1924, while surrounding areas went to the new Yugoslavia.

János Kádár, who led Hungary from the 1956 failed revolution until 1988, was born here, as was Mihaly Csikszentmihalyi, the psychologist of Hungarian background who developed the notion of *flow*, a state of intense and gratifying involvement in work and other activities. It's also the birthplace of Oretta Fiume, who starred in Fellini's *La Dolce Vita* and adopted her hometown as part of her stage name, as well as Agathe Whitehead, the British-Austrian aristocrat and mother of the Trapp Family Singers.

I take my bus to the last stop, in one of the highest points in town.

The first thing that strikes me inside the JPII Center is a long building with doors every few feet. The whole thing is marked *ispovijed*, confession. Twenty priests could hear hundreds in preparation for large outdoor gatherings. I can't help imagining lines of penitents, fingering their rosaries while waiting for the next slot. Concrete slabs divide the individual booths, promising privacy, but I've certainly seen warmer, more inviting confessionals.

I wander a brick path among acacias and oaks, then discover several more walkways curving among the hilly terrain. There are shrines every hundred feet: Stations of the Cross. Of course, you need to start at the bottom of the hill to emulate the road to Golgotha. Some day, maybe I'll do these outdoor stations—maybe as penance following a confession—but for now I'm satisfied to peek in at the Baroque church at the lower end of the complex. Franciscans in brown habits pass me on their way to Mass. Near the entrance, a larger-than-life, polished black-marble statue of JPII at a kneeler faces the church.

Pope John Paul's origins are also Austro-Hungarian – he was born Karol Wojtyła just inside today's Poland across the Tatra mountains from Slovakia. His father served as an officer in World War I under the last emperor, who was beatified as Blessed Karl of Austria in 2004. While remaining a Polish patriot, John Paul had an international outlook, and certainly was instrumental in ending the Cold War and getting Europe together again.

I trudge sloping neighborhood streets, past Italianate buildings with shutters of dark brown and green, until I come to Trsat Castle. Ruins from an old Roman colony gape from the ground below – or are those the fortifications built by the Frankopans in the thirteenth century? Austrian general Laval Nugent von Westmeath, of Irish birth, curiously, bought the property in the nineteenth century and renovated it to its present state, with classical porticoes and a mausoleum where he now rests. A large turreted tower of rough stones looks like it might have been part of the original estate of the Frankopan family centuries before. I climb thirty feet up worn stone steps to find views of Kvarner Gulf all around.

Given the natural sheltering, it's easy to see why Rijeka became the site of the Austro-Hungarian Naval Academy in the mid-1800s. The town is tucked in between the Dalmatian coast and the Istrian peninsula, beyond which lies Italy.

Just across a ravine are socialist-era high-rises, and below lie the docks, with cranes pointing up, like bony fingers gesturing from two miles away. Now, looking almost straight down, I see water running through the ravine – it's the Rečina, or rivulet. This little river lent its name to the normal, non-diminutive form, Rijeka, a full-fledged river.

Dark gray clouds loom, so I find a restaurant table under a broad canopy. But no storms strike and, after a meal of tagliatelle and mussels, I take the bus downtown.

Here I stroll the Korzo, a wide pedestrian boulevard, admiring the myriad of architectural styles. The library is housed in a Hellner and Felmer building, resting atop square pillars of white blocks, their multiple layers looking like thin slices of wedding cake. The mustard-walled second floor has neo-baroque windows, a small balcony in front of each, separated by neo-classical white columns with brown Corinthian capitals. Bronze roofing with a dark patina tops it all, and even there smaller bay windows with decorative molding peek out. Imaginative, like an elevated dollhouse style. Looks so cozy I'd want to rent a room on the top floor some rainy night.

Elsewhere, there's a Roman arch, a Venetian-style palace, a neo-Gothic Capuchin church in brick and white stone. A sumptuous six-story imperial-yellow building with white trim dominates a whole block. A sign reads *Jadrolinija*, or Adriatic Lines, the former Yugoslavia's cruise company, still a state-owned Croatian firm.

The clearest marker of Rijeka's Habsburg past is the Civic Tower. Beneath an austere black and white clock with Roman numerals spreads the imperial double-eagle with a crown over each head. I pass through its gate into the heart of town and, amidst the bustle of café life, I find the Cathedral of St. Vitus, patron of the city who also gives it its German names, Sankt Veit am Flaum or Sankt Veit am Fluss, both of which also derive from the word for river.

It's a fairly simple rotunda, a bit like the mosque-turned-church in Pécs. There's no sightseeing tonight: several women in their twenties are selling tickets to Mascagni's *Cavalleria Rusticana*, to be performed outside. But it's already starting to drizzle. Chorus members huddle next to string players in the church. I'm concerned about the singers' voices: should they try to perform, even if it does clear up?

"I'd like to go, but should I wait or...?" I ask a college-age female in black dress with white nametag.

"You can buy ticket now, and if weather is too bad, we just refund your money."

I take her advice and find a cozy wine bar across the corner. But the luck I had catching the concert in Zagreb despite threatening weather has run out. So I take a cab back to the hostel, riding through the rain. Oh, well, Trieste, which has a reputation for its Habsburg character, now beckons.

* * *

The bus cuts straight across the Istrian peninsula rather than taking the scenic route around the coast. It slows at the Slovenian border as guards wave us through. While Croatia gained EU associate-member status in 2011, Slovenia had already become a full member in 2004, along with the Czech Republic, Slovakia, Hungary, and other Central European countries.

Trieste, called Triest in German and Trst in Slovenian, is essential to this journey, as it was part of the Habsburg Empire from 1382 to 1918. (Much like Rijeka following the First World War, the town and surroundings became the Free Territory of Trieste after the Second, though it was finally divided between Italy and Yugoslavia in 1954, with the city going to the former, the outskirts to the latter.) It was also the residence of Archduke Maximilian, the younger brother of Franz Joseph. A naval officer, he'd been instrumental in establishing the port in Trieste, which became one of the most important in the Monarchy. He later accepted an offer from Napoleon III to become Emperor of Mexico, but he was arrested and executed in 1867 by republican forces after a mere three-year reign. His Miramar (Look-at-the-Sea) palace sits on the Adriatic just a few miles from the city.

Another symbol of the imperial past looks over the gulf from a promontory: Castello di Duino, which once belonged to Princess Marie von Thurn und Taxis. Her name clearly lent itself to Wes Anderson's Madame Desgolffe und Taxis, octogenarian lover of Grand Budapest concierge Monsieur Gustave, the woman who dies leaving the much younger man a priceless painting. The real-life figure, Princess Marie, inherited her title and estate through a Czech branch of the Thurn und Taxis family. She played host—by most accounts only platonic—to poet Rainer Maria Rilke, one of the greatest poets in the German language. An Austro-Hungarian himself, Rilke was born in Prague in 1875. She told him to stay as long as he liked; he strolled the property for several years, drawing inspiration for Duino Elegies and other works.

James Joyce taught English here for nearly ten years while honing *Portrait of the Artist as a Young Man*. Once war broke out, he moved to Zurich, as most of his students had been conscripted. He, like Rilke, died and is buried in Switzerland.

After storing my heavy luggage at the train station, I happen upon a vitrine full of books on World War I. *La Grande Guerra e la Memoria* has a steel helmet on the cover, and a yellowed map of Central Europe, in which Trieste and Trent appear as lonely Italian-speaking enclaves within Austria.

On the street, scooters buzz and swarm around a traffic circle – very Italian. I jog through a break in the three lanes of speeding motorists into a tree-lined area. What's this? A blackened bronze statue of Elisabetta, the empress. Sissi's long hair is neatly coiled around the crown of her head, the remaining locks tumbling over her shoulders. She stands regally as peasants in white granite adore her from both sides. She sailed from here on her noted voyage to Greece where she practiced that language, with much the fervor she'd earlier applied to Hungarian, and indulged in the country's classicism like a Romantic-era poet, though not to the extent of Byron dying for its independence. She often stayed at her brother-in-law's Miramar on her visits to Trieste and was fond of the locals.

This is the first town I've arrived in without reservations. Thanks to the light load, I feel free to wander and search for a place to stay at a leisurely pace. Two blocks down the main drag, I find a room for € 130. Not cheap by my standards, but I'm fatigued and crave a little privacy. And a nap in the AC.

At twilight, I join two hundred locals seated in a city square about half the size of a football field. Behind the stage is an eighteenth-century building with an archway in the middle allowing pedestrians—and historically, coaches—to pass. Common in Venetian architecture, the feature is known as sotoportego. A curious backdrop to the ensemble of electric guitar, upright bass, drums, violin, piano—all played by men in tuxedos—led by a five-foot, balding, hawk-nosed singer in wire-rims. An almost cartoonish figure, his banter evokes bubbly laughter from the crowd. Even with my weak Italian, I can tell some lyrics are in local dialect. He introduces some music as "old Trieste songs." Midway through the show, he lights into *"Gott erhalte, Gott beschütze unsern Kaiser, unser*

Land" (God keep and protect our Emperor, our Land), the Haydn tune that became the Habsburg anthem that became the German national hymn. He stops after the first line, waves a hand, and shakes his head. The audience laughs sporadically. Of course, they're not pining after the old order. But there's no denying the Austrian past. Curiously, it's the umpteenth time I've heard the melody on this trip, but only the first time I've heard those words. And to me, it does evoke nostalgia.

* * *

The name of the main square, Piazza Unità d'Italia, refers to liberation from Austria-Hungary, although local Slovenes still call it Veliki trg or Great Square, as in the old days. It's full of cream-colored buildings, subdued, more Viennese than Roman. Now, at night, lights shine from balconies, windows, and lampposts. Others illuminate façades. More hang on lines at outdoor cafes amid the chatter of diners and drinkers. Blue lights among the cobblestones shine up into the night sky in perfectly regular rows every twenty feet, like landing strips. The municipal building stretches the width of the square, and a clock tower rises from its center, enhancing the symmetry.

This summer, three-sided white cloth boxes have sprung up in a half-dozen places among the old columns and statues. Four feet tall, like silky movie screens on metal poles, they are printed with black-and-whites of Trieste in mourning a century ago. That July 2, Franz Ferdinand's coffin was transferred from the ship—the dreadnought Viribus Unitis—for his return to Vienna by rail.

In one photo, civilians in hats and suits line the way as soldiers and sailors near the harbor stand at attention. A carriage passes between. Another side of the box says:

Trieste 2.7.1914/2014
Franz Ferdinand
I Funerali d'Europa

These are not only the images of a State funeral celebrated in our city a century ago, but also of the funeral
of a certain idea of Europe. The horse drawn hearses
not only bore the coffin of the slain Imperial couple,
but also the lifeless remains of a Europe which, even
if mythologized, had seen the coexistence of peoples,
nations, cultures and religions. These images...still
transmit a sense of wrenching melancholy even today....
[They are displayed] in the hope that *that* Europe will
continue to move forward in the future, guaranteeing
prosperity, unity and rights for its inhabitants. Trieste,
with its past errors and tragedies, is now at the heart
of this Europe.

I shiver with melancholy myself. This expression of reconciliation, among nationalities as well as with history, is what I've
come here for.

The lights and silhouettes of today's buildings mingle with the
images on the thin screens, deepening the sense of continuity with
the past. Another view, taken from a fourth-story balcony, shows
the cortège filing through a narrow boulevard. Yet another, of the
procession passing by a granite sculpture, is placed so that viewers
can compare it with the object on the square. A note remarks that
while many Triestans would have preferred to be part of Italy, they

nonetheless showed up in huge numbers to express sympathy for the slain couple. Elsewhere, the text explains:

> ...two infantry companies... were followed by six carriages of wreaths.... Next came acolytes bearing crosses and members of the local clergy, followed by Bishop Karlin, wearing his mitre and a black funeral cope. Behind him came the coffins of the Duchess of Hohenburg and the Archduke Franz Ferdinand, followed by a long train of officials and dignitaries....

It's remarkable that Trieste presents this event more thoroughly than Sarajevo did the assassination itself. And just as importantly for my quest, I have definitively reconnected with my circuit of Ferdinand's footsteps in reverse – or looked at another way, the route he took as a cadaver: Sarajevo-Adriatic-Trieste-Vienna.

* * *

In the morning I stand for a half-hour in the July swelter to buy my Trieste-to-Vienna ticket for the next day. Direct, unlike the other legs when I've had to make transfers not mentioned in the published schedule.

But when I finally get to the window, the schoolmarm-ish clerk, dark-brown hair in a bun, eyes me over her reading glasses as if I hadn't done my homework. "You have to take a bus from Udine to the Austrian border town of Villach, then board a second train."

"But all the internet timetables indicate a direct train."

"Well, the bus is owned by Austrian State Railways, so it's the same."

Ironclad logic. I resist the urge to roll my eyes. Another Republic of Zubrowka moment.

* * *

In the afternoon, I take an open double-decker bus tour of the city, which covers everything from its Roman ruins to its numerous streets lined by five-story fin-de-siècle buildings, to the hotels, restaurants, villas, piers, and beaches along the less congested northwest shoreline.

As evening approaches, I stroll by cafés and down the quay looking out on the bay, where fishing vessels and tourist boats chug by. Tankers dot the horizon. Not far away is the Canal Grande—much less grand than Venice's—where fifteen- and twenty-foot boats dock at metal posts rising from concrete embankments. One-way streets flank the canal, which runs three blocks up to a domed church with classical portico. I take a pedestrian bridge over the water, as skiffs bob lazily on waves rolling in from the bay. The smell of salt fills the air.

I stumble onto a corner restaurant just off the main square. A short, squat, lively server in white linen skirt and blouse with red waistcoat greets me with wide eyes and smile. *"Benvenuto! Prende la cena fra noi?* Welcome! Are you going to dine with us?"

"Si, d'accordo."

She continues in Italian, even as I struggle with the language. She must assume I know her language better than she knows mine. All other restaurant and hotel staff seem comfortable in English, but I welcome this chance to practice Italian.

"Una bicchiere di vino rosso? A glass of red wine?" she suggests with raised brows and a nod. "Or perhaps a *mezzo?"*

"A *mezzo?*"

"Half-liter."

What the hell, I'm going to rest my legs and watch people go by for the next two hours. I get a soup called *jota*—white beans with carrots, green beans, and other vegetables, meat and a bit of herbs. Cecilia, as I'll call her, hustles away the empty bowl, and hastily returns with the main course. I don't know when I've had such good service at a mid-priced European restaurant, I think as I tackle my gnocchi with mushrooms and sausage. A bit on the greasy side. Smoky. Heavy. Indulgent in a way Slavs would like.

As she takes my plates, I ask, "Is this dish Slavic influenced?"

"*Si, è d'origine slavica.*"

Well, of course, we're only a few minutes' drive from Slovenia. Gotta love that multi-ethnic flair.

I wander the side streets, slightly tipsy, until I come to a tiny park. I approach a statue in the shadows of oak leaves, and find enough light to discern the inscription: Maximilian. Ah, yes, I recognize the beard, parted in the middle, with a long tuft on each side. More of the Habsburg past. Thematically, it segues nicely into my next destination: the old imperial capital.

* * *

The next morning, as I walk through the station to my train, the word *sciopero* appears in yellow lights on an announcement board. When I first started learning Italian, I wondered why the textbook introduced the word 'strike' in chapter one. I quickly learned it's a common occurrence here. Fortunately, I'm avoiding this one by twenty-four hours – I'm expecting enough other complications as it is.

When I arrive in Udine, my transfer station, there's no indication where to catch the bus, no personnel on the platform to consult. I ask a snack bar owner, communicating in gestures and simplified English. He responds in something not quite Italian, probably the local Friulian dialect.

Following his instructions, I trudge two blocks with my thirty-pound backpack, and my guitar, Emilia, in her TSA-approved pristine black case.

In front of the bus station, Slavs, Germans, and Italians crowd around a concrete island, searching for a posted schedule that mentions Villach. We conclude that the bus has to stop somewhere within sight, and it can't possibly leave us all behind.

A rumor circulates that it's an hour late, and we lounge like lizards sunning themselves on the dusty steps. I chat with a Mexican tenor studying in Bologna, now travelling to his next opera gig in Kraków. (Also part of Austria after the Partitions of Poland. I've been there before but will have to pass on this journey.) I have him take a picture of me, the Galloping Gypsy, "riding" the guitar case like a horse.

When the bus finally arrives, the driver starts stowing luggage in the compartment underneath, but he's not giving out claim tickets. I really have no choice but to trust Emilia to Austrian State Railways.

But as we get going I relax. The view of the shallow aquamarine Fella River, flowing over sandy-colored rocks and through Alpine passes, puts my mind at ease, makes the hardship seem worthwhile. It brings back memories of a 1994 bus trip in the opposite direction, when our choir travelled overnight from central Slovakia to Rome, with only short restroom breaks. (In fact, it was in preparation for that trip that I first started learning Italian.) We pulled out pillows and blankets as this vista unfolded at dusk. This time, in late morning, I'm groggy, but refuse to sleep through the scenery. Somewhere nearby is the "trilingual corner"—there is some Slovene population here—where the Slavic, Germanic, and Latinate worlds meet: three major civilizations.

When we arrive at Villach, the driver unloads suitcases, rucksacks, a cardboard box, a massive duffel bag – and my guitar. Travelers bump elbows in a frenzy to grab belongings. The driver, running out of room, sets my backpack off to the side.

I pick it up and beeline across the street, through the railway station to the much-needed WC. As I finish my business and turn toward the sink, it dawns on me: *Where's Emilia?*

I snatch up my things and hustle back. Floor tiles glisten, as do the twenty-foot windows and stainless-steel outer claddings of the escalators. Children hold hands with parents on their way to the platforms. Doesn't look at all like an urban station where thieves prowl. Did I set Emilia down somewhere absent-mindedly? Could someone have made off with her while a partner-in-crime distracted me? I retrace my footsteps to the bus terminal. But just as I reach it, the bright-yellow coach I just took from northern Italy pulls away. I wave my free arm frantically at the driver, twenty feet from his windshield, as he blithely shifts into second. Does he not seem me – or is he trying to make up for lost time? A cloud of dust billows in his wake like smoke in a magician's act. *Poof!* The platform is empty. My guitar has vanished.

I go straight to the office. This is a small town where most folks speak only German. Thank God, I learned my conjugations and declensions thoroughly in college. But now, instead of worrying about masculine and feminine endings, I need to *communicate* quickly and accurately. To locate the guitar, if possible, before it gets permanently lost or stolen.

I address the clerk in German. "I just got here by bus. My guitar is missing."

If his English is better than my German, he'll switch languages, for sure. He continues in his native tongue, and despite my worry, I feel vaguely justified. "I'll call *securitas*."

"Call whom?"

"*Securitas*."

Great, now he's speaking Latin.

A portly man in dark blue uniform saunters in through the automatic door.

"I lost my guitar. Or it was stolen," I tell him. "I'm not sure."

He frowns. "When did you last see it?"

"I just came on the bus from Udine." I catch a breath and tap a finger to my temple. "Ooh, now I remember! The driver set it down. I started to reach for it, then he set my backpack way to the other side."

The guard raises an eyebrow.

I struggle to excuse my stupidity. "I've been travelling for weeks. Must be getting tired. I ran to the bathroom. But how could I have forgotten my guitar?"

He purses his lips sympathetically. "If no one claimed it, the driver would have put it back on the bus, you know?"

"Sure hope so."

Herr *Securatis* punches up a colleague on his cell phone. Then tells me, "The bus isn't at the next stop yet, but should be shortly."

More on the ball than I am, he uses the pause to ask for a description. At least language-class activities and tests prepared me to negotiate situations like this. "It has a black, shiny new case. Just

bought it two months ago. There's a silver strip around the side."
But I feel like a bilingual idiot.

After five minutes, his smartphone bleeps. He listens for a sec,
then repeats my phrases in Austrian dialect. A second's silence. "*Sie
haben's g'funden?*" Ah, a positive note. He turns to me: "They found
it. Sending it back on the next train from Klagenfurt."

I wince. "Uh, sorry. Forgot to tell you. I'm taking the next
train to Vienna."

He sighs and dials his colleague again. After some brief uh-huh's
on our end, he hangs up. "All right, here's what we're going to do.
Get on the train to Vienna. Get on the first car after the dining
car." He speaks slowly – to me, the moron with the advanced-level
German. "When the train stops in Klagenfurt, step off, look around
for an official in a blue uniform." He points at himself. "Just like
I'm wearing. Wave your hands to get his attention if he doesn't see
you. He'll have your guitar."

As we slow toward the Klagenfurt station half an hour later,
I peer anxiously from the narrow window on the carriage door.
When we grind to a halt, a yellow button blinks. I poke it, and the
pneumatic door swishes open. A slimmer version of Herr Securitas
is waiting outside—with Emilia.

"Danke sehr!" I say, clasping the handle, wrapping my other
arm around the waist of her hourglass curves. Could Emilia still
be in one piece? I find a non-occupied area of four facing seats
(compartments are rare in Europe anymore), and open the case
on the Formica table. Emilia is alive and well! I'd like to play her
right now, but in the middle of a first-class carriage? I stroke her
nylon strings gently, close her up, and squeeze down the aisle to
the still-comfortable second class.

11

Vienna Boys: Sigmund, Stefan, and the Habsburgs

I can relax now. Hills and valleys sigh with me in relief, their breath filling the sails of boats scattered around an aquamarine lake. We're gliding along the shoreline at 130 km/h, as a small screen overhead informs us. It's 632 km to our destination. As in an airplane, a map shows the route curling easterly, then northerly, around the Alps to Vienna.

I find a map of the train lines and finally understand the hitch to this leg of my journey: there is no rail through this part of southern Austria and northern Italy. I've travelled from Vienna to Rome and back in a Pullman, but sleeping through it all I never realized: to travel non-stop by train, you go through Ljubljana, capital of Slovenia, around the taller Alps. That's the route the Archduke took. I'll have to set my perfectionism aside and be satisfied that I've done things as thoroughly as I have.

Outside the train window, a church shines white on a hilltop clearing amid dark conifers. We round a bend in a valley and a castle appears atop a promontory. Below the main structure are three levels of battlements with guardhouses. The fortified walls have turrets at each corner, and the sharp steeple of a chapel pokes up from within the ensemble. *The Sound of Music*, tempered by medieval charm.

"What's that fort called?" I ask the businesswoman across the aisle.

"Hochosterwicz. Dates back to the ninth century."

"Is it a museum?"

"No, an aristocratic couple lives there. But you can arrange a visit." I put it on my mental bucket list, as she disembarks at the next station.

Similar vistas open up along the way, but none so spectacular. We slow in the flatter country of Lower Austria four hours later, and pull into Wien-Meidling station in mid-afternoon.

Meidling sounds so similar to Mayerling, a town near the capital where Franz Joseph's only son and heir, Archduke Rudolf, a thirty-year-old married man, carried out a suicide pact with a teenage lover in 1889. Franz Joseph's younger brother Karl Ludwig became heir apparent, but many, eager for a younger ruler, preferred Karl Ludwig's son Franz Ferdinand.

Franz Joseph had also succeeded in similar fashion. In 1848, Europe's Revolutionary Year, students had barricaded themselves in the streets of Paris, Frankfurt, and Prague. When the conflagrations had spread to Vienna, the imperial family had fled north to Olomouc, Moravia. I've visited the very room in the archbishop's palace, full of gold trim and marble busts, with a red plush "throne," where uncle abdicated in favor of nephew, skipping the next in line to give the people a youthful sovereign. Franz Joseph, then eighteen, would rule for sixty-eight years, eclipsing even Queen Victoria's reign.

As I step into a sleek subway car, I get my head out of the clouds of history and sit, backpack still on, computer case wedged securely between me and the window. Though I generally feel safe in Vienna, I stand Emilia's black case on end and hug her firmly between my knees.

Franz Joseph's inauspicious start came as the nation-state ideal was taking hold in an empire of peoples seeking greater autonomy. He ceded considerable territory to Germany and Italy, which had been previously divided into principalities and duchies, but by then were rapidly uniting. He suffered personal loss: son Rudolf, brother Maximilian – and wife Elisabeth, stabbed by an anarchist as she boarded a steamship in Geneva in 1898.

Twenty minutes later I emerge from the escalator into the hall of Praterstern station, a hub linking U-bahn, bus, and tram lines, full of commuters of all ages and classes. I zip past fast food joints till I reach the broad, sunny entrance, step over streetcar rails and around a traffic circle. A red marble rostral column juts up amid electric wires, utility poles, and stoplights. Boats seem to pierce the monolith, their curved ends like figures on a totem pole. Atop it all stands a life-size copper statue of nineteenth-century Admiral Tegethoff.

From there I trudge two hundred yards, with guitar and bags, up the Heinestrasse, named for German poet Heinrich Heine, past four-and-five-story buildings, and settle in to a hostel. It's run by a U.S. university with semester/year abroad programs in the city. The receptionist addresses me in flawless American.

"Do students in your program study the language here?" I ask after the check-in.

"Not intensively. Most don't use it much. All the content courses are in English."

"Yeah, I can understand they wouldn't need it here. Vienna's so cosmopolitan. It's easy to get by on English if you're just here for a year."

"I really wish I knew it better," she adds. "I've been here for a year, and I took it two years in college, but still haven't got beyond the basics. Funny thing is, I grew up speaking Armenian at home. Thought I'd have an advantage at languages."

"If you get far outside of Vienna, it'll definitely come in handy." I recount the tale of my lost guitar. We have a good laugh before I take the elevator to my room.

After unpacking I long to give my nearly-lost guitar more attention, caress her strings, but not here in the noisy hostel. I take her up the Heinestrasse to its end at the Augarten, a large park with a nineteenth-century villa, but the sign on the wrought-iron gates says it closes in five minutes.

There's a similar villa in a similar park that used to belong to Franz Ferdinand's youngest brother, *"der schöne Otto*, handsome

Otto." The dissolute man spent his last weeks there, nursed by his last lover, dying of syphilis at forty-one, refusing to see his wife or mother until a brief farewell shortly before his death. But it was his son Karl, a devout Catholic thanks to his *mother's* (i.e., Otto's wife's) influence, who became crown prince after the Sarajevo assassination.

A lone woman pushes a stroller outside of the Augarten, glances in my direction, and soon moves on. So I strum Emilia on a green wooden bench and play a song from *The Czardas Princess*. Kálmán began composing the operetta—wistful but with a happy end—in late 1914, as Austria-Hungary was going to war. It premiered in December 1915, in both German and Hungarian libretti. A prime end-of-the-empire symbol. Kálmán himself was also emblematic, in particular of the Jewish population which thrived so well after Franz Joseph granted them total emancipation in 1867. (It is said that Hitler liked Kálmán's operettas so much that, after the Anschluss, he offered to make the composer an "honorary Arian," but the composer refused the insult and emigrated, first to Paris, then to the U.S. So his works were banned in the expanded Third Reich. I haven't found the original source of this story and regard it as apocryphal.) His tunes are rife with Slavic and Gypsy musical influences. When Roma friends in Košice, Slovakia, would play it in restaurants, I'd join in. The Slovak-Romani-Hungarian trilinguals got a kick out of me, the American *gadjo* (non-Gypsy), singing the Magyar version of these old favorites.

Since I've left my lyric sheets in Sarajevo, I'm trying to reconstruct the text in my halting Magyar, stopping between lines to write. Rhythm and melody, those ancient aids to memory, help me string out the words:

Nem él jobban kinában, sem a kinai császár

Mint mikor a szívemre, a bubánat rászáll.
[I don't live well in China, I'm no Chinese emperor
Like when the drumroll pierces my heart.]
The vocal part swings high, full of longing:
Magamat nem nyuzatom, szivemet sem zuzatom
(Something about my heart again, the meaning's unclear to
me, but it fits the meter.)
After the words, "I'll just call the Gypsy," the melody dips and
slows, lingering before launching into the brighter, accelerando
refrain, which rolls off my tongue:

Hajmási Péter, Hajmási Pál [the Hajmási brothers], the
barometer stands at rain/Don't worry my rose, it doesn't
matter a grosch [dime]/There will always be grapes and
soft bread/Hajmási Péter, Hajmási Pál, the barometer
doesn't impose/I get that into my head and jump into
the string bass, Hajmási Péter, Pityke Pál.

What a whimsical ending!
The gate to the Augarten clinks shut, and the groundskeeper
walks away.
After a three-block downhill stroll to the hostel, I find sublime
sleep in my bed, with Emilia tucked safely under the frame.

* * *

In the morning I join cyclists, pedestrians, clunking
streetcars, and autos on the *Ringstrasse*. All orbit the city center
on marked paths, passing the university, the neo-Gothic city
hall with its limestone spires, the parliament building with its

neo-classical columned portico. Between the twin Art History and Natural History museums Empress Maria-Theresa stands atop a large pedestal, with various eighteenth-century dignitaries on the lower level, extending her scepter as if to say, "All these realms are mine." Just inside the wide semi-circle of the Ring Street, on the *Heldenplatz* or Heroes' Square, a triumphal arch forms the main entrance to the Hofburg castle complex, the nerve center of the old empire. Travel writer Bill Bryson remarked that space aliens seeking the human leader would land here – it just looks like the world capital.

I follow horses clomping down the wide lane leading to the main residential palace.

The "New Wing" arcs out before me, and a sign announces this year's special exhibit, Franz Ferdinand's World Tour. The journey he took three years after becoming heir presumptive, following the suicide of his cousin, Crown Prince Rudolf.

I enter and climb a staircase of white marble with matching balustrades on each floor. Columns of white with veins of dark gray stretch from the railings to the next floor. I imagine tuxedoed aristocrats at dress balls a century ago, taking a break from dancing, hanging out here and looking across the airy interior at partygoers on the other side.

The Ferdinand display snakes through several third-floor rooms, none quite large enough to have been a ballroom in the Habsburg days. The nine-foot wood-and-glass vitrines, about a century old, reach half way to the ceilings.

Faded wall maps show various legs of the trip. A black-and-white video titled "Franz Ferdinand's Journey from Trieste to Yokohama" shows the archduke with Indian and British dignitaries on the steps of a building, then on horseback for hunting. A silky screen bears his diary entry of 20 December 1892, from Port Said: "The mania to buy things, which so easily grips the traveler in foreign lands, is strange. He feels himself pressured to acquire every triviality, whether beautiful or ugly, even horrible trumpery, just to bring home something characteristic of the particular place." I nod, recalling his possessions at Konopischt. That feeling still grips wealthy, fanatical collectors. And many tourists. Unlike His Highness, I don't have steamer trunks to fill, but the docent says I'm free to take flashless photos. So I snap digital souvenirs of Ferdinand's stuff: cymbals, ceramics, necklaces, grotesque ceremonial masks, horns, tapestries. A stuffed kangaroo and wildfowl, doubtless some of his nearly three hundred thousand kills. Numerous weapons, including rifles from his sojourn in Japan, fill a three-sided corner display case.

These reminders of his violent temperament are followed by a diary quote on the "primitive" appearance of bush people, which gives me pause. At least the temporary exhibit balances this prejudiced comment with something from the more humane side of his character:

> [It is] not the desire to behold strange pageantry and exotic splendour...[that] have driven me to remain far from my homeland nearly one long year [but] instruction from personal observation of other parts of the world..., from contact with foreign cultures and people, with alien culture and customs...., from the contemplation of unfamiliar nature and its inexhaustible charms."

It seems an old-fashioned, upper-class multiculturalism combined with shallow exoticism, the good intention that can suffer from unconscious patronizing.

Most of the Germanic bigots of his day considered Hungarians superior to Slavs, though of course not quite as civilized as themselves. And although Ferdinand's plan for greater Slavic autonomy may seem to have been a liberal endeavor, it's doubtful he really regarded Slavs as equals. His visit to America, the last leg of his world tour, partly inspired the idea by offering a model of federalism in action, but by many accounts, his "decentralization" was intended to divide and conquer. More autonomy for Prague, Zagreb, and Kraków meant a relatively weaker Budapest – and a stronger Vienna.

Near the exit, I find a quote from Karl Kraus, the acerbic Austrian journalist, from shortly after the assassination:

> "Of that which his life kept silent, his death speaks, and the half-mourning of the weak cries it through all the streets.... He was not one to greet. He had nothing of that 'winning manner' which soothes a people of spectators at their losses.... A brazen messenger from old Austria, he sought to awaken a sickly age that it not sleep through its own death. Now it sleeps through his."

I sigh. It seems neither Franz Ferdinand nor his dynasty was meant to go on much longer.

Back out on the balustrades, on a wall poster, the archduke peers out of those deep eye sockets underscored by the arcs of his handlebar moustache. Perhaps I've found the real Ferdinand, not the naïve image I arrived in Europe with a month ago. Still,

I feel a spiritual kinship with Franz the traveler. My own, much smaller journey is ten days from finished.

In the two-hundred-foot passageway through the center of the Hofburg, a horse-drawn tourist carriage clomps and rattles through. The old guardhouses are now a ticket office and souvenir shop. Sandwich boards advertise the Spanish Riding School's Lipizzaners and Court Chapel Masses with the Vienna Choir Boys.

In the traffic circle behind the Hofburg, bikes are locked to racks, a few cars are parked at curbs, and more fiacres roll by. The air smells of horses and manure more than auto fumes. A brown and yellow sign points to a gift shop down a side street: *Vienna Time Travel*.

Vienna *is* time travel, I chuckle to myself.

At the National Library, also part of the historical ensemble of imperial buildings, a huge poster displays a garishly colored bust of Franz Joseph: cantaloupe-colored face, including hair and muttonchops—he was mostly bald at the time of war's outbreak—officer's tunic, normally pigeon blue, now turned cerulean, and a purple background. *AN MEINE VÖLKER*, reads the exhibit's title. "To my peoples," meaning the nationalities of the empire. It's the salutation of the public announcement of war on Serbia.

Inside, white marble columns with gilded Corinthian capitols rise near fifteen-foot wooden bookshelves with movable library ladders. Waist-level wood-and-glass vitrines hold faded posters and documents whose fonts contrast with the purplish-blue, computer-printed display boards behind them. There's an obituary in Italian from the Jewish community of Ragusa (Dubrovnik) honoring the archduke and his wife. This positive symbol of the old monarchy's multi-ethnic character clashes with a satirical map from 1904,

"Austria-Hungary in the Cockle-Doodle-Doo Projection." Somewhat like a barnyard illustration for a children's book, it depicts members of the various nationalities, such as a Ruthenian peasant and a poor Jew from the northeastern part of the empire, both seeking revenge on a Polish landlord. Elsewhere, propaganda posters abound. Some promote war bonds, others encourage farmers to collect beetles to use as chicken feed to save grain for the troops. Displays and commentary stress concepts like the *Erbfeind* or "hereditary enemy," here a reference to Russia. I've just been reading Stefan Zweig's complaint about slogans like *Gott strafe England* or "May God punish England."

While the depictions of war fever may be accurate, the exhibit seems the work of "Habsburg-haters," Austrians who show their dedication to the Republic by repudiating everything about the old dynasty. Here, the concept of Mitteleuropa is stressed as a strengthening of ties between Austria and Imperial Germany, rather than a common Central European heritage embracing Slavs and others. How unlike the commemorative banners in Trieste! The present displays even shine a negative light on the last emperor, Karl, nephew of Franz Ferdinand and grandnephew of Franz Joseph. The Catholic Church beatified him as Blessed Charles of Austria in 2004, largely for his attempts to negotiate an end to the war. These exhibit organizers cast doubt on his secret overtures to France, which he denied when rumors of them began circulating. For this bit of arguably necessary lying, he gets blame, rather than credit for seeking peace.

* * *

In the evening I take a tram along the muddy waters of the Donaukanal. The vehicle eventually crosses the northern bank to a park. I get off and approach the Prater, the enormous pedestrian stretch with its Ferris wheel and other rides. It's a menagerie of cotton candy and popcorn smells. BB guns pop away at a shooting gallery full of stuffed animal prizes. Hm, maybe twelve-year-olds like to come here and pretend they're Franz Ferdinand on safari.

I wonder what this working-class neighborhood, Leopoldstadt, was like in its largely Jewish, pre-World War II days. Freud grew up here after his family moved from his North-Moravian birthplace. Restaurant signs greet diners in a mix of High German and Viennese dialect – *Servus! Griass di in Englischem Reiter* (Ciao! Welcome to the English Equestrian).

I sit at a table next to the main pedestrian drag, for better people-watching, and order a Wienerschnitzel. Soon I'm quaffing a hoppy brew. The server brings the veal on a plate big as a charger. The cutlet has been hammered so flat it's hanging over the edges. I cut off a jagged corner and hold it in the air a moment—the fried, breaded crust is piping hot, with burnt grease odor. Fresh out of the pan, crunchy outside, tender meat inside. Potato cubes, fried golden, round out the meal, along with a small garnish: thin tomato slice, a puny portion of lettuce with a smattering of shredded carrots and cabbage.

When I lived in the Czechoslovakia of the early nineties, I used to get this kind of meal all the time – for lack of menu options. Chicken, pork or beef cutlets, breaded or "natural." I used to think it was an "East European" thing, but it's nearly as common in Austria. I used to get sick of all the meat and potatoes, desperately sought more veggies. But for now, I'm satisfied with the old-fashioned stuffing.

I wander past the Ferris Wheel to the end of the Prater, where people line up for fast food at a poorly lighted and dirty atrium. A small group of men in jeans and dusty plaid shirts stand around a man playing an accordion. They speak accented German, but the musician sings a language I don't recognize. Perhaps Romanian. The area looks a little seedy, and I'm afraid that, in shorts and polo shirt, I'm too obviously a tourist. So I move on.

At the corner of the Heinegasse, I step into a pub with its doors open onto the street. The TV blares its coverage from Brazil: the World Cup final. Germany leads Argentina one to zero. Three couples, sitting around a black-red-and-gold flag spread over a table, watch intently as an Argentine rally fizzles and time runs out. The Germans shout, hug, and clink beers. The Viennese regulars here seem sympathetic – it's the first time a European team has won in the Americas. Or maybe it's that old Mitteleuropa connection.

Although I've been so caught up in history that soccer seems like background noise, it has been a constant, if subtle, companion on this trip. It's kept me in touch with modern times. But then the German anthem starts, and I'm singing the old Austrian *Kaiserlied* to myself once more.

In another couple of days, I'll be indulging in nostalgia with old friends. Catching up on their current lives will also keep me anchored in the present.

* * *

Back at the hostel, I'm assigned a new room. I'll be sharing it with an Austrian female. As I enter the new sleeping quarters, she introduces herself as Stella, a recent geology grad starting a job in town. She spent last summer in the U.S. Her accent is slightly German, but sounds more like American English than British, though she likely learned the latter in school.

But when I unzip a bag and pull out Stefan Zweig's *Die Welt von Gestern*, she switches to her language. "You must be very serious about learning German." Her eyes widen, dark blue. Contrasted with black hair and fair skin, they make her as exotic as a northern European can be – at least to me, an Anglo-Saxon on every branch of my family tree I've managed to trace thus far.

Pushing aside thoughts of attraction, I tell her about my present tour and the years I lived in Slovakia.

"Have you travelled much in Austria? Other than Vienna?"

I recount the bus trips with Slovak choirs and other travels, to the Wachau wine region on the Danube, to the Kaiservilla in Bad Ischl where Franz Joseph used to hunt – and where he signed the declaration of war on Serbia. To Eisenstadt, where Haydn worked as court composer and conductor, or Kapellmeister, for the Hungarian magnates, the Esterházi family.

"I've never been to that part of Austria myself. Hm, used to be part of Hungary. I grew up in Innsbruck, but my mom's from Hamburg. Those two dialects are radically different, so we always spoke High German at home."

Austria is culturally very different from northern Germany, more Catholic and traditional. People aren't so businesslike. Not every inch of lawn has to be trimmed, not every inch of masonry has to be neatly painted. As I just observed on the Prater, things tend to be tidy, but not obsessively so. More fastidious than the Czechs or Hungarians, but not so much as the rest of the German-speaking world. Seems their centuries of close contact with Slavs, Latins and others have worn off on them, mellowed them. It's said they like wine and laughter more than other Teutons.

Stella resumes a movie on her laptop, head propped on pillows, and the conversation trails off. So I kick back at a desk with Zweig's *World of Yesterday*.

Already halfway through, I've read his childhood recollections in the first chapter, called "The World of Security." The reference to pensions and disability insurance guaranteed by the state sets the reader into the mind frame of an age when human progress seemed inevitable. His Viennese *Gymnasium*—or lyceum—offered a weighty curriculum but encouraged little critical thinking. Yet "outside was a city full of a thousand-fold excitements, a city with theaters, museums, bookstores, a university, music, where varied surprises awaited one every day." It was a city where people had high expectations of singers; the death of a beloved soloist would put the whole town into mourning. He and his schoolmates satisfied their "pent-up desire for knowledge, intellectual, artistic, and sensual inquisitiveness, which found no nourishment in school." He and classmates would slip Rilke into their Latin books to read on the sly.

Repressed sexuality was the city's open secret. Corsets and bustles exaggerated the female figure to the point a man might not know a woman's true shape until their wedding night. Legal but regulated prostitution was an outlet for unhappily married males. Freud was a natural product of this environment (though he was born in a small town in northern Moravia, called Freiberg in German and now Příbor in Czech, his family moved to the imperial capital when he was just a tyke).

Completing his studies at the University of Vienna, Stefan added a doctor title to the Zweig name, the first in his Jewish industrialist family to do so. Intellectual achievement, rather than money, he writes, is the ultimate dream of such families. In this, he was a bit like Freud, son of a struggling wool merchant.

Zweig then worked as a journalist, poet, novelist, and play-wright, travelled to Paris, Britain, India, Italy. He got to know Rilke when they both lived in Paris, and the Belgian poet Verhaeren took him to Rodin's atelier there. Zweig later introduced Freud to Salvador Dalí in London, correctly believing the psychoanalyst would be interested in the artist's take on unconscious wishes and desires.

Zweig curiously claims the policies of Vienna's notorious Jew-baiting mayor Karl Lueger never affected him. That may be true, but rhetoric reinforces attitudes, which affect policies. While Franz Joseph's 1867 emancipation of Jewish subjects may have ended discrimination by the state, anti-Semitism persisted in other institutions. The University of Vienna, for instance, refused to promote Freud to full professor because of his background. But to be fair, Franz Joseph despised Lueger, and twice refused to install him as mayor after he won city elections. After a third victory at the polls, according to regulations, the emperor had to give in to the democratic will.

Most members of Zweig's generation had expected the progress of the nineteenth century to continue unabated. But he began to have doubts in 1913, when he met writer Roman Rolland. Zweig often gushes about artists' dedication to their work, but he spares nothing in praise of Rolland. He met Rolland in his Montparnasse "chambers stuffed to the ceiling with books." The prolific author, according to Zweig, walked with a hunch, ate little, and avoided most pleasures but music—of which he had a profound mastery, but no notoriety—and spent most of his hours working tirelessly. In his presence, Zweig continues,

"I sensed ... a human, moral superiority, an inner freedom without pride, the taken-for-granted freedom of an independent soul. At first glance I recognized in him—and time has proven me right—the man who was to be Europe's conscience in a crucial hour.... [He said the] time had come to be alert, and ever increasingly so. The powers of hatred were more vehement and aggressive, because of their baser nature, than those of reconciliation, and there were material interests behind them that in themselves were less scrupulous than our own."

Later that year, Zweig became even more wary of imminent war thanks to the Redl Affair. Colonel Alfred Redl, chief of army intelligence, had been caught selling secrets to the Russians, who, at least according to press reports, had learned of his homosexuality, blackmailed him, and then paid him well. The ploy worked, so the story goes – he developed a taste for luxury and continued delivering info to support it.

When Redl was found out, high-ranking officers pressured him into putting a bullet in his head. This Prussian practice and sense of honor had crept into unofficial Austrian military culture despite its clash with Catholic teaching. In a 1985 film entitled *Oberst Redl*, by the well-known Hungarian director István Szabó, Franz Ferdinand and Franz Joseph are depicted as approving. While the film fairly portrays the decadence of the late empire, including the inflated sense of honor inherent in dueling, the pressure to commit suicide on the part of the devout Habsburgs amounts to caricature. In reality, the emperor was by all accounts appalled that the man was forced to take his own life. (After his son Rudolf's suicide in 1889, he still held out hope that it had not been a damning act. According to Catholic doctrine, it would have had to have been carried out with full knowledge and consent of the will in order to be a mortal sin. While that allowance wasn't given much weight back then—suicides were typically refused burial in holy ground—an exception was made for Rudolf. The archduke had shown signs of depression following a concussion resulting from a fall from horseback. And of course, he was royalty.)

Ludwig Winder, a Jewish Austrian from Prague, wrote in a biographical novel *Der Thronfolger* (The Successor to the Throne, never translated into English), that Ferdinand would have preferred Redl be offered a last confession – then a swift execution by firing squad. That sounds more like the archduke.

In any event, a good portion of the army was on edge over the Redl Affair. According to some accounts he info he'd passed on to the tsar's army ended up costing Austria thousands of men on the Galician front – the Russians knew their every move in advance. There was too little time before the war to redraw the plans. In our day and age, we can easily sympathize with the plight of Colonel Redl, a gay man in a world with little understanding of his orientation. Some sources named his betrayal as the greatest in human history, but more recent research has indicated that the plans he sold had little effect on the outcome of combat operations.

* * *

The next morning, I go to a café with antique wooden tables, newspapers on bamboo holders allowing for easy page turning, and officious wait staff. I make breakfast on Dobos Torte, a sponge cake with chocolate buttercream between its dozen thin layers and caramel glaze. It's named for the Hungarian confectioner who introduced it in 1885 – Franz Joseph and Sissi were two of the first to taste it. I also order the local classic, coffee with whipped cream. Typical Viennese *Kaffeehaus*: service is slow and humorless, but you can sit and read for hours for the price of one cup. It's said that in 1913 Tito, Lenin, Trotsky, Freud, and Hitler could have sat in such a place and looked at each other over their gazettes.

I wander through the Volksgarten where, then as now, ordinary folk stroll near the Hofburg. I stumble on a black-haired man playing Brahms' Hungarian Dance No. 5 on a small hammer dulcimer. After a handful of tourists applauds and drops money in his case, I step up to greet him.

"I from Romania," he replies in broken German.

"I play similar music on guitar. You know *Csardasz Princess?*"

"Sure." He lights into *"Das ist die Liebe,"* a snappy tune you could polka to. I sing along on the refrain.

He smiles and raises a brow as he sets down his sticks. "You want to sing with me?"

"Sure."

"Meet me here at ten tomorrow. Bring your guitar, we'll see what we can do together."

"Will do."

I pass through the Hofburg main gate. A sandwich board on the cobblestones advertises, among other numbers, the "Radetzky March," the marshal music with snare drums, brass and woodwind, that always gets the crowd clapping. It's the standard final piece at the Vienna Philharmonic's New Year's Day concerts. Johann Strauss the Elder composed it in honor of Field Marshal Joseph Radetzky von Radetz (a nicely redundant Slavic-German name for a Czech nobleman), who defeated the forces of the Risorgimento in today's northern Italy in 1848 and 1849. Yet today, Italian audiences are as likely as anyone else to tap to the beat; most modern Europeans have forgotten the song's reactionary origins. Curiously, Johann the Younger composed an ode to 1848's student protestors in Prague. Here, the cognitive dissonance of Austrian history crops up between father and son.

A kilometer down the street the Jewish Museum offers a special exhibit for the centenary, *Unser Kaiser/Our Emperor*, which takes a tack nearly the opposite of the anti-Habsburgism I saw in the National Library display. A flag of the Dual Monarchy hangs from the ceiling, red-white-red stripes of Austria abutting the red-white-green of Hungary, the respective coats of arms in the center of each half. An old photo shows Emperor Francis Joseph I visiting Sarajevo, with a rabbi to the left of Muslim dignitaries. The caption to another picture says Emperor Karl I visited numerous Jewish communities in Galicia, c. 1917. As in well-known portraits, he appears in modest, trim moustache and short-brimmed, cylindrical officer's cap typical of the era. Gloves off to shake hands, he leans his gentle, pensive face, with slightly knit brow and wispy smile, toward two rabbis.

In a video, a goateed historian seated before a bookcase says, "The Austrian crown lands and Austria-Hungary were the first European countries in which Jewish soldiers could serve." (That was back in the nineteenth century, well before the Great War.) Black and white headshots of prominent WWI Jewish soldiers are displayed on narrow yellowish floor-to-ceiling banners, among them, the modernist composer Arnold Schönberg. Another is Joseph Roth, author of *Radetzky March*.

Roth grew up in Galicia, the part of Poland that had gone to Austria in the late-eighteenth-century partitions, which had a sizeable Jewish population. He attended the lyceum in Lemberg, as it was called then in German, and Lwów in Polish, now western Ukraine's L'viv. Despite pacifist leanings, he interrupted studies at the University of Vienna to enlist in 1916.

Radetzky March belongs to the troika of Jewish-authored elegiac works on Austria-Hungary, the others being Robert Musil's *The Man without Qualities* (first volume over a thousand pages, the second never completed) and Zweig's *The World of Yesterday*. In a forward to his own novel, Roth wrote of Austria-Hungary:

> "I loved this fatherland. It permitted me to be a patriot and a citizen of the world at the same time, among all the Austrian peoples also a German. I loved the virtues and merits of this fatherland, and today, when it is dead and gone, I even love its flaws and weaknesses."

Like Zweig, Roth was aware of the stultifying authoritarianism, and of the decadence of the moribund late empire, and these themes color the story as much as its supranational spirit. It begins with the northern Italian campaigns that spawned Strauss' ode to Radetzky, and readers hear that music every time they see the title. An officer saves the young Franz Joseph from enemy fire, and the young emperor ennobles him for the deed. The book then follows this officer and two more generations of men of the Trotta family, all of whom serve in the imperial army. The grandson leads a life of gambling debts, dueling, and affairs with married women – while never marrying himself. All the men drink slivovitz, the schnapps so ubiquitous even now in the former Habsburg realms, and whose name derives from the Slavic for plum. After war breaks out, the grandson is killed on the Galician front while trying to get buckets of well water for his troops. It seems to me a strange redemption—"I was thirsty and you gave me to drink"—from his profligate life.

Roth was driven to alcoholism in the years after the collapse of his homeland – especially after Hitler's Anschluss left him a stateless Jew, compelled to wander the earth like so many forebears. His wife suffered from schizophrenia and was later killed by the Nazis. He is said to have converted to Catholicism, although no one has produced a baptismal record. An apocryphal story about his final days has it that he met Otto von Habsburg, heir to the Austrian throne, in Paris in 1939. Recognizing that the writer was boozing to death, Otto told him, "As your emperor, I command you to stop drinking." Roth complied and, without the alcohol to kill the germs, died of pneumonia several days later. While both fictional and medically unsound, the tale is nonetheless rich for its depiction of two Austrian exiles from disparate backgrounds.

Steeped in nostalgia, I find a restaurant patio with a view of St. Stephen's Cathedral to try Franz Joseph's favorite dish, also Freud's. One of the few things they had in common. A Jewish friend from the States, who's been following my travels on Facebook, recommended Tafelspitz, boiled beef with applesauce and horseradish. While I'd prefer a salad for lunch—I'm not losing weight on this trip, despite all the walking—I have to have it, just this once. At least this version comes with diced yellow peppers, adding vitamins as well as color. The meat is tender, slices like veal. I have the server take a picture with me, the dish, and a brochure from the *An Meine Völker* exhibit. The old emperor's garishly colored face and uniform—the same as on the poster I saw yesterday—add hues to the photo.

I return to the area of the National Library where I saw *An Meine Völker* yesterday, to Lobkowicz Square. It's named for a nobleman of Polish origin – and for the Lobkowicz Palace that now houses the Theatermuseum. A marquis outside quotes Zweig: "I no longer identify with my own ego." The exhibit, *Abschied von Europa/*

Goodbye to Europe, is a nod to the author's observations on a Europe that had begun falling apart in 1914. Perhaps the renewed attention from *Grand Budapest Hotel* also has something to do with its timing.

Inside the palace's atrium, a huge skylight illuminates a wall-sized black-and-white of a steamship. A lengthy passage from Zweig's *The World of Yesterday*, stretches out from the photo on a carpet. But instead of the Star Wars intro titles, "A long time ago, in a galaxy far, far away...," it begins in German, "Week after week, month after month, more and more refugees came to England."

The exhibit's main room is full of boxes packed for moving, emblematic of his final departure from the continent in 1941. Many of them hold framed pictures that visitors can flip through like a stack of posters in a shop. Portraits of the mustachioed, bespectacled Zweig alternate with those of other authors, such as Franz Kafka, of Zweig's wife, and of the Salzburg villa where they lived from 1919-34. They left for London after the Anschluss. A highlight of that stay was delivering the eulogy at the funeral of Freud, who had also fled there. Older relatives stayed behind. As Zweig noted in *The World of Yesterday*, a point also made in the Jewish Museum, Viennese Jews were denied use of park benches in Vienna, a harsh prohibition for elderly people out for a walk. That capital of the old empire "degraded to a provincial German city," as he'd put it in his foreword.

Zweig chronicles the rise of National Socialism from its goon squad days to Hitler's chancellorship. In early 1933 the writer inadvertently caused a stir in Germany. Posters for his play *Burning Secret*, which was due to open soon in Berlin, naturally evoked chuckles from passersby the morning after the Reichstag fire. Nazi officials drove around in jeeps methodically tearing them all down by noon.

While the regime incrementally passed laws stripping Jews of their rights, not all their works were immediately banned. An exhibit on the second floor of the Theater Museum illustrates the point. It's about Richard Strauss (a German composer unrelated to the Austrian Johann) and seems timed to coincide with the one on Zweig (though it has more to do with the composer's one hundred fiftieth birthday). Strauss was named president of the Musical Chamber of the Reich in 1933, for which history has often denigrated him. Yet he used his position to hire Zweig as librettist for his opera *Die Schweigsame Frau* (*The Silent Woman*) and stuck to the Jewish writer's text for the 1935 debut. Party leadership expressed disapproval but didn't force the composer to find a new lyricist. Still, they only let it run for three performances, and Strauss was soon pressured to resign.

In addition to Zweig's status as an undesirable in his homeland, his UK travel papers designated him a "hostile alien" when World War II broke out. He was afforded better treatment in the U.S.: on display are the opening pages of the second draft of *The World of Yesterday*, then in 1941 under the working title *Blick auf mein Leben* or "A View of My Life." He donated this manuscript to the Library of Congress in gratitude to the many town libraries in the U.S. which had lent him materials.

This exhibit suits my exploration of the vanished world, only I wish there were a different ending. Zweig, living safely in Brazil but despairing of Europe ever recovering a culture of decency, committed suicide with his wife in 1942. The day before, he mailed the final manuscript of *Die Welt von Gestern* to his publisher. If only he had waited three more years. Of course, even then, he would have had to have endured a Europe separated by the Iron Curtain. Who knows how he would have taken it?

Outside, in the back of the Hofburg complex two men in black pants and maroon shirts—apparently the casual uniform of the Lipizzaner trainers—guide a line of white horses through the street, going home after a day's work. Going out the main entrance, I notice that a black and yellow, i.e. Habsburg colored, sign announces "K.u.K. Souvenir's," using that abbreviation for "Imperial and Royal." Except that the red-white-red flags with double-headed eagle are republican: the bird holds a hammer in one talon, a sickle in the other. (The symbol merely expresses solidarity with workers and peasants, and is not exclusively communist.)

In the Volksgarten, I pass a Sissi statue that I saw in the morning, this time noticing the Austrian Imperial Crown carved in relief on white marble. Past and future meld. Although I haven't had time to indulge in modern art on this trip, I know that, in spite of its reputation for living in the imperial past, Vienna also has its avant-garde, its artistic future. The Vienna International Centre sprawls just north of the Danube, housing the International Atomic Energy Agency, several major UN offices, and the International Commission for the Protection of the Danube River. The city's university is home to one of the world's leading translation schools. Wind turbines stretch from the plains to the east into Hungary, with no noticeable break at the border. Vienna will maintain its relevance well into the future.

* * *

I return to the Volksgarten the next morning, guitar in hand, but see no hammer dulcimer player. Of course, I didn't really expect him to show promptly at ten, but now I wonder how serious he was. A Slovak friend is coming to pick me up in three hours, but I thought it'd be nice to make music, maybe get some tourists clapping along. Tips would be nice, too, but I'm not sure I can legally earn them here. Buskers can play in other parts of town unrestricted, but in the center you need a permit, acquired by appearing at a certain office on a certain day of the month to audition.

I wait fifteen minutes on a park bench, warming up my voice and fingers, but still no Romanian guy. I put Emilia back in her case and shuffle along a gravel walkway, to wait at the spot where we met yesterday. Now I'm almost hoping he won't turn up – I'm just too uneasy about playing illegally, and being late for my ride. I sit at an out-of-the-way bench and play quietly another twenty minutes as passersby cast curious glances and move on. Not psyched for public performance, I leave after another half hour.

I have just enough time to visit the Capuchin Crypt, or Kapuzinergruft, where Habsburg rulers of the last couple of centuries are buried.

"You can't take your guitar in," says the lady at the ticket window.

"Can I stow it here?"

There's no coat check in the small entrance, but she opens the booth and squeezes it in behind her seat.

It's cool and silent. I pass seventeenth-century archdukes and a couple of emperors before coming to the magnificent baroque bronze sarcophagus of Maria Theresa, topped with cherubim. Then there's the somewhat more modest grave of Franz Joseph, flanked by wife Elizabeth and son Rudolph, his only male heir who committed suicide in 1889.

There is no grave for Franz Ferdinand here. The final humiliation he and his wife suffered for their morganatic marriage was the denial of the usual imperial honors for her burial. It's said Franz Joseph's chamberlain, who had a grudge against the archduke, influenced the emperor in this decision. Franz Ferdinand chose a final resting place beside her, in the Artstetten Castle in Lower Austria. For all his faults, his love was true.

For Franz Joseph's grandnephew and successor, Charles I, there is only a bust in a corner, at the level of my chest atop a column. This "Blessed Karl of Austria" was exiled to Switzerland in early 1919. He'd signed a declaration acknowledging the dissolution of Austria-Hungary as such, but never abdicated. In the tumult following the war, Hungary went through a one-month stint as a Soviet Republic. Soon after, Miklós Horthy, an old Austro-Hungarian admiral, assumed the position of Regent of Hungary. (He maintained the post until 1944, when the hard-core fascist Arrow Cross Party ousted him despite his alliance with Hitler.) Karl made two ill-timed attempts to claim the throne of Hungary, and was finally exiled to Madeira, a Portuguese island over three hundred miles from the Moroccan coast, in late 1921. He caught pneumonia the following spring. As he lay dying, he received last rights, and insisted that his son Otto join his mother to witness his final breaths to see how a Catholic dies. Karl is buried on Madeira, another prospective pilgrimage site for me.

English writer Herbert Vivian anticipated the Catholic Church's 2004 beatification by nearly a century when he wrote:

Karl was a great leader, a prince of peace, who wanted to save the world from a year of war; a statesman with ideas to save his people from the complicated problems of his empire; a king who loved his people, a fearless man, a noble soul, distinguished, a saint from whose grave blessings come.

Between him and Franz Joseph, next to the wall, lies the wood and copper casket of the last person buried here, Karl's son Otto von Habsburg. I last saw it in 2011, the year of his death. He'd passed away in July at ninety-eight and had received what will probably be the last state funeral for any Habsburg: a Haydn requiem Mass, including homily by Vienna's Cardinal Schönnborn, the old Kaiserlied, a procession around the city center, a twenty-one-gun salute, and finally, entry into the Imperial Crypt. The last included the tradition of Habsburgs interred here: A man knocks on the door in his stead, and a Capuchin monk in brown habit responds, "Who desires entry?" The officiating layman responds for the deceased with name and titles: Prince of This, Duke of That, etc. "We don't know him," comes the answer. After a second knock, the deceased is represented by non-royal accomplishments such as, in Otto's case, president of the European Parliament. Once again, "We don't know him" is the response from within. Then comes a third "Who desires entry?" The final answer is "a sinful, mortal man," followed by "Let him enter."

I linger for a moment by the casket, remembering what Otto did to help reunite his family's old realms. In 1989, he and a Hungarian politician arranged a "Pan-European Picnic" on the frontier between Austria and Hungary. The border gates were to be opened briefly, symbolically. East Germans had gotten wind of the event and showed up, pouring through and overwhelming the guards. Over the next few weeks, the Ossies kept coming, hoping the liberal gesture would be repeated, and eventually many more were allowed through Austria to West Germany, precipitating the fall of the Berlin Wall.

I actually owe a lot to Otto, for I wouldn't likely have come to this part of the world, fresh out of college in 1990, if it hadn't been for those events.

I retrieve the guitar, then glance at my watch. Oh, my God, it's already past noon, and my buddy from Slovakia is supposed to pick me up from the hostel at one!

12

A New Look at Old Stomping Grounds in Slovakia

I dash to the U-Bahn and wait impatiently for the next subway to the Prater. Marian texted me yesterday that he'd be in Vienna, so I asked him for the favor. Being late will look like I'm taking him for granted.

Marian played viola in an ensemble with cimbalist Alena

and two Roma: Alex, violinist and leader, also called a *primas* in various languages in this part of Europe, and a rotund bassist, Jožo or "Joe." Nowadays Marian runs an expediting service, a more regular source of income, and drives his van from central Slovakia to Bratislava several times a week, occasionally coming to Vienna, a four-hour trip.

I see his white van, a five-year-old Renault, sitting outside the hostel. He hops down from the driver's seat. Wearing a tee shirt, he smiles, the chiseled features of his solid chin and head accentuated by close-cropped blond hair. He gives me a firm handshake and introduces me to his son, Maroš, a wiry, dark-haired sixteen-year-old.

He and Maroš stack my large bag and guitar on top of cartons in the back of the van.

Calling Alex by the familiar name, I ask Marian, "How is Šaňo, by the way?"

"Quite well. He's founded a school for the arts. Helps disadvantaged Roma kids. He's married to a Belarusian."

I recall a picture of Šaňo, thick black curly hair and bushy eyebrows, southern-European looking, as much as anything. He's in white shirt and black open vest, a typical "uniform" for restaurant musicians in Central Europe. Marian and two other musicians stand nearby. Seated next to Alex, in a gray suit, is Otto von Habsburg, bald nonagenarian in large round glasses. Behind him is a blue flag with twelve yellow stars in a circle. It was 2004 – he'd come to congratulate Slovakia on its accession to the EU and was also en route to Sarajevo for the ninetieth anniversary of the assassination.

Marian drops off a large cardboard box at a small agricultural business in a village. We then cross the border, barely noticeable thanks to Slovakia's EU membership. Barely noticeable except that things look more polished in Austria, dustier and a bit shabbier in Slovakia. The Austrians must think Marian's labor cheap, and the prices they are willing to pay, higher than the going rate in Slovakia, are nice for him (though his gas and maintenance costs are the same as elsewhere in the EU). Soon we're stuck in Bratislava's rush hour traffic. We finally turn off into a neighborhood of stone cottages, wending our way past parked cars on the narrow street. He throttles and strains at the wheel, trying to back into a driveway. Then he and son carry an eight-foot bookcase from the garage to the van. I offer to help but they refuse, tilting it to make it fit. He's determined to make every mile of this trip pay – I suppose he has to.

We're soon back on the open road, where willows and poplars line a river snaking through the Carpathian foothills. The same scene as when I first arrived in Slovakia—via the Vienna airport—and three teachers from Gymnázium Tótha drove me in a Škoda to my first job in the town of Martin. Only then it was mid-October and the colors were blazing.

Marian's smile sinks into a frown as he struggles to downshift on an uphill grade. "Damn clutch is overheating." We reach the peak, coast down the other side, and at the bottom he grinds into third as we prepare for another climb.

On the next descent, he pumps the clutch.

"What for?" I ask.

"Helps keep it lubed."

Doesn't make sense to me, but – whatever. We soon pull into a convenience store for gas, sandwiches, and a much-needed cooling-off.

I ask about Alena, the hammer dulcimer player in the old band. He says she lives in Poniky, a village outside of Bystrica. He gives me her number, and I call her on my tiny Nokia. I tell her I'll be in town and we agree to meet.

Soon the clutch is acting up again. He pumps it on every downhill stretch, more frantically each time we coast. Finally, an hour later, we reach the flat valley of the broad, slow-moving Hron. No more shifting for the last twenty minutes of our journey. We enter Banská Bystrica's city limits and follow the bend in the river around a two-hundred-foot hill covered in pine and fir. Urpín it's called – I had a view of it from one of the many socialist high-rises for fifteen months when I lived in this neighborhood. As we roll into downtown, Marian curses every red light. Finally, he turns onto a bridge, puts the van in first, and limps up to a tiny parking lot at the end. He calls a repair shop on his cell and says he'll get it towed tonight and fixed tomorrow. This may be a setback, but his business seems to be doing well. Except for the clutch, this vehicle is in much better shape than the twenty-year-old East-Bloc clunker he was driving the last time I saw him, in the late nineties.

He and Maroš help me with my bags to the Národný dom hotel just up the street, which fortunately has vacancies.

After check-in, shower, and nap, I go the rest of the way to the main square. I pass through an archway, in a building with windows overhead, like the *sotoportego* in Trieste. Then it all comes into view. Black granite obelisk to fallen Red Army soldiers, the statue of the Virgin at the top of the long, narrowing pedestrian zone, clock tower behind that. All around are shops and restaurants in renaissance buildings, painted in lime, salmon, mauve, and yellow. Café tables spill out onto the cobblestones, which were lain during the summer of 1994, between my first and second years living in the town. A fountain sprays into the air, its burble mixing with the whispers and laughter of diners and shoppers, and the occasional shriek from toddlers. A large part of the pleasant urban atmosphere that kept me here for three years. I stroll up the square to where it narrows into a street with more stores, offices, and bed-and-breakfasts. I come to a corner building with a small dome, covered in fish scale-pattern tiles, atop its third story. I sigh. Just like in Zagreb or Budapest.

I turn back and go to the *Zlatý bažant*, or "Golden Pheasant," the restaurant where I spent hundreds of hours listening to my friend Alex and his band back in the nineties. Little has changed but the music: now a keyboardist sings a medley of folk songs on the patio. The menu still has the chef's invention, a crepe filled with cubed chicken in a creamy paprika sauce, a nice twist on the traditional Hungarian meal. I order it for old time's sake.

A man of mixed Latino and African background, with guitar case, enters the gate. He tunes up and joins the other musician, who taps out steel drum sounds on his synth. I chat with them during a break. The guitarist is Cuban and knows little Slovak or English, so I try my halting Spanish. Another of Otto's languages.

"I play with a Latino band in the U.S." I tell him.

"What country of origin?"

"Mexican. We mostly play Mass in church, occasionally do weddings or quinceañeras."

"So you know '*Cielito Lindo*'?"

I nod, and during the next set, I'm ay-ay-ay-ay-ing my heart out. As do the other twenty patrons sitting outside. After a couple of Slovak numbers, they have me sing "Yesterday." But I don't need a place to hide away; I'm doing fine living the moment.

* * *

The next afternoon, Alena and I wind around a mountain road in her ten-year-old Skoda. Her round face is accentuated by her black hair pulled back into a single braid. She so looks the part of the Slavic villager when she wears a folk costume, linen with floral patterns, and sits at her instrument, the cimbal.

"I'm successfully divorced," she says. I don't know the details of the marriage, and she doesn't volunteer more info. So I don't ask. Motioning her head to the back seat, she adds, "This is my son, Tomáš."

I reach behind me to shake hands with a dark-haired ten-year-old.

As we enter the village of Poniky, Alena points to a steel-and-glass building front with the name Kooperativ. "This is the one business that's survived the *prevrat*," she says, using the word for overthrow. "The farmers were totally self-sufficient until 1989. Then they let everything fail and sold it off." I'd never known Alena to talk like a communist, but maybe she's become upset at how things have turned out in the last twenty years. And she is an old school teacher, so she well may have been a party member, but never let on about it back in the nineties.

"So what do you think of the situation in Ukraine now?" she asks.

"Well, Crimea is majority-Russian, so one can argue it never should have gone to Ukraine in the first place. But Putin's way of taking it, sending in green men, just makes it a diplomatic problem. Most of the world will never recognize the annexation."

"But I mean Kiev. Those people who took over, they're fascists."

I sigh. "About twenty percent of the new government are nationalists. That makes me uncomfortable. But the other eighty percent are not fascists."

"As far as I'm concerned, they're *all* fascists. Every single one."

I guess next she's going to tell me the Malaysian Airlines flight that was just shot down was all Ukraine's fault. Never mind that it was over rebel-held territory and it had all the hallmarks of falling to Russian-provided weaponry. Guess it depends on which echo chamber you're in. Not wanting to argue with my host, I change the subject. "So when did you move to Poniky?"

"Ten years ago. I've got a small place, but it's finally fixed up the way I want. I'll show you, but first I'm taking you to a fourteenth-century church. I made a special arrangement with the vicar."

We wind to the highest hill in town and stop outside a three-foot stone wall surrounding the building. A friar in brown habit, with long pointed hood hanging down in back, greets us at the gate, a ring of bulky iron keys in hand. As he swings the massive wooden door open, its hinges squeak. He explains that the renovation took place in the 1970s and eighties. A remarkable accomplishment given the suppression of the Church at the time, but the priest in charge made the case for the building as historical landmark.

The inside walls are covered in frescoes. St. Mary, Protectress appears in soft blue hues in a corner. The Last Judgment is against a black background. In one scene Satan, as prosecutor, disputes over the deceased while Jesus and Mary plead for his soul to God the Father as St. John the Evangelist looks on. In another scene, called the Living Cross, the right hand at the end of the crossbeam blesses Ecclesia, the Church, holding a banner and chalice. The left hand stabs Synagogue, for reasons I don't understand represented by a blind-folded woman standing atop a donkey.

"This stems from a time," the monk half-mutters, eyes cast downward "when even the Franciscans were involved in persecuting Jews."

Yes, *even* the Franciscans, the order formed by the peaceful animal lover of Assisi. It seems no one is immune to the prejudices of a given day and age.

But our guide stretches an arm proudly forth to point out the triptych over the altar. Its center is a blocky Byzantine-style cross, with ultra-wide beams; images from the lives of Sts. Nicholas and Barbara adorn the two wings. "St. Barbara is widely honored in this area as the patron of miners."

I've been to numerous mining towns in Central Europe and have seen lots of St. Barbaras. Banská Bystrica's name derives from the word for mine, as does Banská Štiavnica, whose mining academy was the first in the world. Kremnica, about an hour away, used to produce silver ducats known all over the world. But most of the wealth went to Hungarians and Austrians, not the poor Slovaks who worked the shafts.

Outside the church, we stand at the stone wall surveying the hilly countryside with its quilt work of fields, forests, cottages, and barns. A warm breeze wafts over us. The friar fingers the keys. He hands me a brochure on the church in English. "You can read about it in your language if you didn't catch all my talk."

"Thanks. I couldn't quite process all that history in Slovak."

"I never had an ear for languages," he says. "I lived in Africa for ten years, only needed English for basic communication."

Alena, Tomáš and I say goodbye and go to her place, a whitewashed stone cottage with black slate roof. The windows are deeply inset—it dates to the nineteenth century—but the flawless glass panes and the wood in the frames are clearly new. In her living room, a mere ten by fifteen feet, sit an antique rocker and a stove with glazed tiles – plain white, though I've seen decorative ones with hunting and courtly love scenes in castle-museums in this part of the world. On the yellow walls, in the corner, almost nestled under rough-hewn beams, five deer antlers, a ram's head and a stuffed pheasant complete the rustic atmosphere.

"You didn't shoot them yourself?" I joke.

"No, I got them from friends or bought them."

"Nothing to rival Franz Ferdinand's collection."

She laughs along – his penchant for hunting is well known in this part of the continent.

We have a cup of tea sitting on a lawn plot not much bigger than her living room. Her son finds a four-leaf clover. I go over to look at the bulky steel door that gates her stone fence – it too is about a hundred years old. It's folded back against another wall; when I look behind it, I start. Two gray bats, each smaller than my hand, are sleeping there.

The three of us then go to a restaurant called *Koliba*. The name refers to a traditional shepherd's hut, but this is a much larger building on the highway north to the town of Martin. Inside, servers in linen shirts with cross-stitched floral designs scurry between kitchen and tables. Even in summer, a wood fire burns in a large, open, central hearth. Its smoke drifts up into a copper hood, shaped like an upside-down funnel, which tapers to the ceiling thirty feet overhead. More folk costumes line the pine-slate walls, as do icons of Jesus and his mother and other saints at the bottom of the tall, gently sloping ceiling.

We sit at a wooden bench and table and order from the menu. Not many vegetables on this one, either. I suppress my health-food obsession and go with old-fashioned comfort food: sausage balls wrapped in doughy pillows. Smoky, greasy, with bits of mushrooms, washed down with a hoppy local lager. Not bad, but I wouldn't want to eat like this every day.

Alena, Tomáš and I take pictures of each other. Alena gets one with me standing under a pair of antlers so they look like they're growing from my head. It's the old joke about cuckolding, but I'm not married, so it can't *really* apply to me.

Alena drops me off near my hotel room in Bystrica. It's been great to reconnect with people like her and Marian, but it appears I won't get a chance to see Šaňo the bandleader on this trip. Nor the choir Hron, named for the river flowing through the town, that I sang in for three years. But another choral reunion is in the making for tomorrow's destination.

* * *

The next morning I take the 10:30 train to Košice in East Slovakia, my last stop before Prague. Not far from Banská Bystrica, a white castle called Ľupča looms over a hillside from within its gray stone fortifications. Used to be yellow, back when I attended a folklore festival there. A recent renovation is nearly complete, with red tin roofing here and slate there, but some rough stones and chipped masonry still haven't been spackled over.

The track flattens to a slow-moving river surrounded by reeds and, beyond its banks, cottages. A stork soars, then air brakes to light on a nest of thick twigs wedged between the chimney and the black shingled roof.

Soon the train is sitting in a railroad yard full of box cars and rusty fences. I open *The World of Yesterday* to distract myself from the ugliness. In early August 1914, Zweig was in Belgium, just as diplomacy had broken down. Hmm. Franz Joseph had signed the declaration of war in his Bad Ischl mansion and summer residence called the Kaiservilla. Someone had placed under his nose a document claiming the Serbs had fired on Austrian troops as they were mobilizing just across the Danube, in what was then a part of Hungary called the Voivodina. The reports were frauds. But it seems Franz Joseph was determined to deal Serbia a punitive blow, and the bombing of Belgrade began the next day, July 28, exactly a month after the assassination.

Germany and Russia declared war on each other three days later, and France and Germany did so on August 3. Zweig believed himself in a safe position in Belgium. Even after all the disillusionment he'd suffered in recent months, he couldn't fathom that Germany would violate Belgian neutrality to invade France. But, warned by friends that he should get home before hostilities started, he got a ticket on what turned out to be the last civilian train headed east. It stopped between the two countries' border posts. In the darkness he could make out the silhouettes of tarp-covered artillery on flat bed cars. As he alighted at the German station, police directed passengers outside. The platforms were off limits, but he could hear boots clomping and officers' sabers clinking on the concrete.

In a few minutes, my train starts up again. Around two I arrive in Košice. A half-dozen platforms shelter under a tin roof, just off the main building, and I have to take a pedestrian tunnel under the tracks to get inside. The East Slovak "metropolis," as local media call it, has a population of nearly a quarter million. It used to be Hungarian-majority and known as Kassa (Kah-sha) in that language, as Koschau in German and Cassovia in Latin. In 1939, in concert with the arrangements that gave the Sudetenland to Hitler, a southern swath of Slovakia was adjoined to Hungary. Admiral Horthy, the post-Habsburg regent of that country, famously rode into Kassa on a white horse, to the hurrahs of local Magyars. But after the war, the communist government ramped up the steel industry, and the influx of Slovak workers left the Hungarians a minority in the town.

As I trudge with my belongings down the hall, passing travelers arriving from various parts, I catch snippets of conversation in Ukrainian—or Ruthenian, the tongue of a very small East-Carpathian minority—I'm not sure which. They are poorer than their Slovak counterparts, with clothes that look overused and under washed, hair that could stand shampooing. They could be from Ukraine for all I know, or from less developed areas of Slovakia.

Despite the poverty, I wish I could have made a trip to L'viv, Ukraine. It's the Lemberg of Joseph Roth. And of Leopold von Sacher-Masoch, who lent his name to masochism – there's even a café in his honor. Lwów, as it's known in Polish, had belonged to Galicia, the territory annexed by Austria in the Partitions of Poland. After the First World War, it became the scene of ethnic violence among Poles, Ukrainians, and Jews. Nowadays, it's often said to be home to the most nationalistic Ukrainians – the ones Alena and other Russophiles consider "fascists." And there is some truth to that. As much as I'd like to visit L'viv for historical reasons, it'll have to wait for another trip.

Right now it's more important to catch up with old friends. When I moved here in 1996, after three years in Banská Bystrica, Šaňo, the Roma violinist, put me in touch with Viliam Gurbaľ, Košice's cathedral organist.

"We played together in the army," he'd told me. "Me on violin, Vilo on *cimbal*. He leads a really good cathedral choir. You should join."

It turned out to be the best choral group I've ever sung in, with a repertoire from Renaissance to modern sacred music. These musicians rarely belabored vocal parts, just heard the harmonies once on keyboard and pretty much knew it – or just sight-sang straight from the sheet music. Half of them were conservatory students or graduates. Others were part-time opera singers in Košice's National Theater.

I tramp to a local bed and breakfast, only about six blocks from the station. But along the way, I make a sudden turn, pulling a muscle in my back. Oh, no, stabbing pain, with stiffness immobilizing part of my torso. Just a week to go on this trip, and I *have* to slow down.

My room is just across from the conservatory, a couple of blocks from the cathedral, and one block from the practice rooms of the St. Cecilia chorus. I store my bags and head to a Friday-afternoon rehearsal, another routine from years gone by. I take the coach entrance to the eighteenth century building and catch Vilo, dark hair becoming salt-and-pepper, just before rehearsal.

"Marku!" He addresses me with a dialectal Slovak vocative case, which is somehow always endearing. "So glad to see you!" Vilo invites me to join the choir the next day when they travel by coach to Banská Štiavnica to sing Mozart's *Requiem*, a special Mass for the dead of World War I. I'd love to visit the UNESCO heritage site, and I've sung the *Requiem* with them before and know most of the bass part by heart. But my exhaustion and back pain force me to decline.

I stay with him as rehearsal begins. Chamber musicians are also part of the act, and soon we're going through the familiar, if somewhat dark, passages of the *Requiem*. The deep bass vibrates my chest, the bassoon warbles its low but climbing notes. The singers make their entrances smoothly, notes clean. Still Vilo stops and calls for a more gradual crescendo on that phrase. As we start singing again, I look around and notice a sign saying 1914-2014. They're going to display it at their performance. As we finish the movement, I spot a two-foot crucifix above the window and think of the twenty million dead in World War I. The final words of the *Requiem* come to mind: "*Dona eis requiem. Et lux perpetua luceat eis.* Grant them peace. And may light eternal shine upon them."

* * *

After rehearsal, we pour out into the street. A few of us share stories of our lives since we last met three years ago. Some go home to their families. Ten of us continue to the *korzo*, the central pedestrian zone, a half-mile long, bulging in the middle around the cathedral and tapering on its northern and southern ends. From among the dozen restaurants with outdoor seating, we choose a pub with lacquered oak tables and benches. Soon we're elbow-to-elbow clinking froth-topped mugs.

A band of four Roma, with bass, two guitars and fiddle, stands outside the waist-high picket fence surrounding the pub's sidewalk tables and start playing East Slovak folk tunes. All the choir members, and some of the other patrons, join in the singing.

"Do you know 'O *poštaris*'?" I ask when they finish.

"Sure." They light into it, and I stand alongside and sing. They seem delighted I know the Romani lyrics. The crowd claps along, and some give the musicians a few one-Euro coins. The violinist narrows his eyes at the smallest tips, his lower lip poking out.

When I sit back down, Vilo frowns. "They didn't ask *you* for money, did they?"

"No."

"No?"

"No."

Vilo's played with Gypsy musicians for years—and we have a dozen mutual friends of that race—so I can hardly accuse him of racism. Maybe Vilo's just learned to pick out the good from the bad.

Many people in this part of the world don't acknowledge the existence of "good Gypsies." Košice, in addition to its Hungarian and Rusyn populations, also has a lot of Roma. Maybe twenty to thirty percent of inhabitants. Hard to tell: census takers are frequently afraid to enter their neighborhoods, and many poor Roma don't associate with the *gadje* or outsiders. Those who respond to questionnaires often self-identify as Hungarian. Many speak that language, considering it more prestigious than Slovak. Yet there are enough educated "elites" who do socialize with *gadje*, that three years ago, I often sat at sidewalk cafes and drank with Gypsy musician buddies, and not a single server batted an eye.

We Cecilians drink a second round and part with hugs and handshakes.

A block away, I peek in at the Hungarian theater bar. (Hungarians *and* Roma have their own theaters in this city.) Three years ago, I hung out here after every Cecilia rehearsal. We'd sing along as two young Gypsy brothers would play, on piano and bass, everything from Viennese favorites to "Sway." Sometimes a cousin would pop in around midnight, after playing in the opera, and add violin. But the place is dark and silent this evening.

I saunter almost to the end of the *korzo*, when I hear the guys I sang with an hour ago. I sit down with them at a café table and sing "Yesterday," then a spirited Slovak drinking song. They're rhythmically and melodically spot on. Can play almost anything by ear. I could get along with them, I think, when the fiddler, says, "All right, you don't get this accompaniment everywhere. Not for free."

I lay a five-Euro bill on the table.

He smirks. "C'mon, you can do better than that."

Deep in my gut, I'm livid at the arrogance. My vague suspicions about his earlier reaction to "small tips" were right. "Nope. Nope. Sorry, fellas. That's all for tonight," I say in clipped phrases. These musicians are talented enough to get restaurant gigs for pay plus tips. Other *Romale* do it in this town. So why don't these guys?

I walk away without looking back. I'm reminded of a colorful but tragic 1977 Soviet film, *Gypsies are Found Near Heaven*. It's set in the Carpathians, a bit east of here, in the Austro-Hungarian empire of 1900. One of the lead characters warns his son about people from another camp. "They're the wrong Gypsies." He scowls. "They trade horses for gold." Vilo *was* right. These are the wrong Gypsies. Just in it for the money – but apparently without the discipline of scheduling shows and being on time.

* * *

I wake up the next morning with my back aching. The curtain flutters by the open window. It was still warm when I went to bed at eleven, but now cool air is gushing in. That's not helped the muscles I pulled yesterday lugging my stuff from the station. As I stand, my lumbar region tightens. I can only walk leaning forward. I lie on my stomach and arch slightly, hoping for some release, but it helps very little. At breakfast, I try sitting in various positions, but nothing is comfortable.

At least I know of a reputable Thai massage establishment towards the other end of the square. They book me in an open slot two hours later. After that, I'm at least not wincing. I spend the rest of the day either lying in my bed or eating at restaurants on the *korzo*.

Sunday I wake up feeling much better. I go to the nine AM Latin Mass, less than a block away in the cathedral. The bulky wooden door on huge black iron hinges is unlocked. I climb the worn, uneven stone stairs and find a dozen friends from Gregoriana, a new choir that broke off from Cecilia when its schedule became too demanding.

When I was last here in 2011, many walls in the church were covered with scaffolding and drop cloths. Now all the off-white bricks are clean. The whole interior is much brighter. The sun shines through the stained-glass windows behind the altar with medieval triptych. In a side chapel are windows depicting Francis of Assisi. Next to it, is a scene from the life of St. Elizabeth of Hungary—or "of Thuringia," as Germans call her—the Elizabeth for whom the cathedral is named. One legend has it that she was carrying bread for the poor, bundled in her apron, when her husband, who disapproved of her charitable activities, spotted her. He demanded she unfold her apron, and the bread turned to roses. She smiled and said they were for him. Francis and Elizabeth were namesakes of the imperial couple, Franz Joseph and Sissi, and the Latin inscriptions in a lower pane indicate that the windows were a gift from them. A coat of arms in the Magyar colors red, white, and green—a mountain with three rounded peaks on one side, double cross on the other—is a reminder that Franz Joseph was Apostolic King of Hungary. Blue and white diamonds on a shield under Elizabeth indicate Sissi's

Wittelsbach heritage – she was of the Bavarian royal household.

We choristers form a semicircle behind the stone balcony railing for the offertory hymn. I join in since I know the Renaissance work from years past.

A chandelier with several circular rows of lights hangs suspended from the ceiling on a fifty-foot cable, seeming to levitate in the middle of the cavernous space. Atop it is another reminder of the past: a gold crown of St. Stephen, with its cross tilted slightly. Legend has it the original was once dropped, or the lid of the chest housing it was clamped down too tightly, but there has never been any attempt to "fix" it. It sat in Fort Knox after World War II, and following decades of diplomatic wrangling was returned to Budapest in 1988. It has been on display in the Hungarian Parliament since 2000. Now the hallmark of Hungarian statehood, its image is widely used on emblems, on flags, on money – even though that country is a republic. The actual crown once sat on Franz Joseph's head, as he underwent the coronation ceremony in 1867, the year of the Ausgleich. In 1916, his successor Karl wore it in his only public coronation, as Apostolic King of Hungary. He had to undergo the ceremony in order to open the parliament in Budapest. During the war, there was no time to bother with an imperial coronation in Vienna.

After Mass, we singers wind down the spiral renaissance staircase and then saunter down the street for the ten o'clock brunch, just as in years past. Bells boom and clang as worshippers stroll and push baby carriages to the ten-thirty Slovak-language Mass. At noon, there will be yet another in Hungarian. At least these things never change here. But some of my old friends now have toddlers in tow. Or preteens eager to get out from under their parents' shadow.

After we say goodbye, I move my things from around the corner to a slightly better pension. At least this bed-and-breakfast, so the guestbook tells me, was good enough for Andrea Bocelli when he gave a concert here a few years ago. The owner has quite a collection of glass and crystal, displayed on glass shelves backed by mirrors, with track lighting, in the restaurant and lobby. Like many of these artisanal pieces, the building itself dates back to the eighteenth century. The renovation modernized some of the interior, but kept the white-washed stone walls intact, and preserved the cellar, which is also viewable though glass flooring, museum-like.

I decide to drop in on the noonday Mass in Hungarian for old time's sake. I understand the homily only vaguely, but the music aids my memory as I sing along on the Creed and the Our Father.

In the afternoon, my back is still a bit sore, but not tied in knots like yesterday. So I walk a mile from the center to see the new museum quarter. The conversion of Warsaw-Pact-Era barracks was, like Vilo's musical projects involving the transcription of eighteenth-century musical manuscripts, one of the things that won Košice the City of Culture honor for 2013. The four-story former sleeping quarters have small windows—almost prison-like—but they've been painted cream, contrasting with the black metal roofing and gutters, and with a black granite sculpture, a rectangular block, on the sidewalk. Large grassy spaces add color, as do the hundred-foot oaks, with their leaves and bark, as well as the shadows they cast, giving everything a chiaroscuro effect. Inside one of the four main buildings, I find paintings like a mix of abstract art and manga, such as one called "Cloud Atlas." In this surreal work, darker, lower levels of nimbus are capped by layers brightened by the sun; all this towers over a background of blue, black, and purple mountain peaks, with a foreground of a cerulean stream bordered by dark gray earth – or is it volcanic ash? A sign indicates the exhibit is supported by the EU's Regional Development Fund.

I wander around the complex and notice foot-high wooden stages under some of the clusters of trees. They're only about twenty feet square, apparently for smaller, more intimate performances. The sign in front of a one-story, glass-fronted building offers such a gathering, coming up in just fifteen minutes, part of a month-long series of literary readings, with Scotland as honorary guest. I order a bottled Budvar and find a seat among the fifteen audience members, thinking it'll be nice to get some culture in my native tongue. But, alas, the Scottish author has called in sick. Instead, there will be a poet from Brno. No one leaves upon hearing this announcement, so I guess I'm the only Anglo among them. I try to ignore my aching back and focus on the Moravian Czech. While some of the vivid writing—and occasional profanity—sink in, I'm missing a lot. If I'm going to enjoy Czech poetry, I need to read it first.

Back in the center of town, I wander around, gazing down at the numerous pavement tiles around the cathedral, reading the names on them. Andrea Bocelli earned his place here with a donation to the renovation. Nearby, I find the slab from Otto von Habsburg's visit. 1999. The year after that, I met his daughter Gabriela. Just after Putin came to power – and she pointed out that his KGB background did not bode well for either Russian citizens or the West. I gave her a CD of music by the St. Cecilia choir. I hope it left some impression on her about what these artists from her family's poorer, former eastern realms were accomplishing with their talent.

I call a few friends to try to find someone to hang out with, but all are busy with family, getting ready for the upcoming work week. Guess my last full day here won't exactly go out with a bang, so I decide to make an early night of it and get plenty of rest.

13

Back to Prague: Hello Roma Musicians, Goodbye Empire

I board the Eurocity train for Prague in the morning. It's about the longest route in the former Czechoslovakia. We're soon gliding by rivers and a dam. After an hour and half we're climbing in elevation toward the Great Tatras, just tall enough to have streaks of snow at the highest peaks now in July.

On the northern slopes is Poland, the part that Austria took over in the Partitions. John Paul II was born there between the world wars; his father had served in the imperial army under Emperor Karl. It was also to that region that Stefan Zweig, the pacifist, travelled as a war correspondent. He writes in *The World of Yesterday* that he went there on one of the many trains transporting fresh troops to the Galician front. Returning to Vienna on one of those bringing back the dead and wounded, he encountered an elderly priest who had run out of oil for performing last rites on the young men. "I am sixty-seven and have seen much," the cleric said. "But I would never have believed such a crime on the part of humanity possible."

Four hours into the journey, we pass through the Czech-Slovak border. As they're both EU countries, there's nothing to mark the change, but right about this time the cold front I've been reading about online brings a torrent of rain pelting the roof and windows. When things calm down from the initial burst, I fall into a gentle snooze.

A couple of hours later, we stop in Olomouc, where Franz Joseph became emperor. I spent three summers and an autumn taking classes at Palacký University, just around the corner from the archbishop's palace, and would frequently stop and read the plaque on the wall indicating that this was where he'd begun his reign. I regret I won't be able to get off and revisit. As we pull away, I have to be satisfied with a view of the copper onion domes on the corner towers of Hradisko, a small monastery. Quaint, but a mere side attraction in this, the Czech Republic's second most important town architecturally.

We pull into Prague in early evening. I put clothes for three nights in my "carry off" and stow the large backpack in the left luggage office. My guitar is light, shouldn't cause any back problems. The rain has stopped, leaving only quiet dripping from trees outside the station. But halfway to my final hostel stay, it starts again. I could pull out my umbrella, but it's not worth it in this mere drizzle. Instead, I dash from one shop awning to another along the way, colliding with oncoming pedestrians trying to do the same.

Tired of bumping elbows, I pause at a hair salon. Through the plate-glass windows, the glow of the lamps on the two customers' heads and their apparently convivial conversations with the stylists seem homey. I haven't had a cut in five weeks – seems like a good time for one.

I wipe my shoes on the rug inside. "Do I need an appointment?"

"No. Please, just wait five minutes. You can set your things down," says a petite hairdresser in accented Czech.

I sit on a thinly cushioned sofa and leaf through a tabloid until she's ready.

Once I'm in her chair, she asks, holding a tuft of hair between middle and forefinger, "How much do you want me to take off?"

This reflection in the mirror seems mighty familiar, a repetition of hundreds of haircuts, yet I struggle for the Slavic words to say, "Just a centimeter – and a half. Leave a bit over the ears."

Detecting my unease, she says, "You can speak English."

"But I want to practice my Czech. Or did I not speak clearly?"

"Well, yeah, but, I actually speak English better than Czech. I'm from Albania."

"How long have you been living here?"

"Eight years. I'm surprised you know Czech at all."

I explain my background in Central Europe, getting that goosebumpy-sleepy sensation as her fingers run through my hair, nails grazing my scalp. A nice pampering, like my massage two days ago. When it's done, the rain is over again.

I trudge with guitar and bag, a bit reluctant to move at all, through streets now glistening under street lamps. I cut a diagonal across the high end of Wenceslas Square to another alley.

In front of an eighteenth-century building, the umpteenth such I've seen on this journey, renovated countless times in the past two hundred fifty years, I find the name of my hostel next to a row of buttons and ring the bell.

"Who is it?" comes a voice, crackly, through a mini-speaker covered by an index-card-sized chrome plate. After I speak my name, the solenoid buzzes on the heavy wooden gate, made for coaches to pass through. Twenty feet inside the vaulted entrance is the door to what turns out to be a small suite of rooms. In the reception area, a half-dozen college-age kids slouching on white leather sofas divide their attention between a widescreen and their smartphones. The clinking of dishes and smell of tomato sauce emanate from a kitchen through a door at the far end. There must be twenty people crammed into this place. So much for comfort.

I wait to check in at a cubbyhole just inside the entrance, where a thirty-year-old receptionist, a man with yellowish skin and curly black hair, sits in a swivel chair at a computer monitor. Pigeonholes, manila folders, and papers climb to the ceiling. He finishes dealing with a younger blond female in French, then commences a brief phone conversation in halting Czech.

That done, he asks for my passport in English. After scanning the photo page, he explains, "You'll need to leave a deposit of seven hundred fifty Czech crowns. It's for security."

I hesitate, then he continues, "Don't worry. I'll give you a receipt."

He puts the cash in an envelope and files it away. After he escorts me into a semi-occupied room, I plop my stuff onto a lower, vacant bunk bed. Despite the wall AC unit, I feel the humidity, from guests showering and cooking pasta, as well as from the weather. Even after an hour of hanging out, checking email, and sorting through my belongings, the dampness never dissipates.

Out on the street, just a block from Wenceslas Square, I realize how touristy the area is when I buy food from a Chinese shop owner who speaks English poorly and Czech hardly at all. He doesn't need the local language for communicating with the international kids from the neighborhood hostels.

Back at my lodgings, I eat a cheap supper of rice, pork, and vegetables. Francophone students wander in and out of the kitchen. Although I've been to Prague many times, I've never been in such close contact with such a wide range of nationalities in just two hours. The Czech capital today is probably more cosmopolitan than fin-de-siècle Vienna ever was. As a showcase of Romanesque, Gothic, Baroque, and Art Nouveau architecture, it has more attractions. At least for the eye – musical Vienna holds more pleasures for the ear. Prague is the millennium-old seat of the Kingdom of Bohemia. Vienna only superseded it once the Habsburgs definitively settled down on the Danube in the seventeenth century, after Holy Roman Emperor Rudolf II had held court in Prague, inviting, among others, the astronomers Tycho Brahe and Johannes Kepler. Rudolf's legacy includes many colorful stories of alchemy, as well as the legends surrounding his friend, the Rabbi Loew, namely the lore about the Golem, the gorilla-shaped clay figure who comes to life and can be controlled under certain conditions, which vary from story to story.

With these thoughts in my head, and amid expectations of tomorrow's museum visit and a meeting with a musician friend, I find sleep in my dark, cramped room among eight snoozers.

* * *

The next morning, I go to the National Museum. The three-story building at the high end of Wenceslas Square has, on most of my visits, served as little more than a backdrop to the equestrian statue of the Bohemian patron saint of that name. The ninth-century duke, Václav in Czech, who morphed into King Wenceslas for the English carol, holds a lance with a pennant near the tip, with a pointed helmet atop his head. Four other saints stand on the corners of the plinth below him. At least the patina of the museum's roof matches those of the figures.

In a pedestrian passageway, leading safely under a busy street that cuts the museum off from the square, a shopfront bears two-foot-tall, stylized Cyrillic lettering: СКАЗКА – "fairytale." Signs in Russian and Czech advertise specialties like Stoli and red and black caviar. There are roughly thirty thousand Russians living in Prague, a number that has steadily climbed since the 1990s. Some Czechs welcome this community; others complain of growing mafia influence. The Czech president, Social Democrat Miloš Zeman, is cozy with Putin.

As if to show the conflicted attitude of this society to their presence, a kiosk just outside the underpass displays Czech newspapers with a negative article on the Kremlin leader. The front-page photo is of a woman holding a sign with Putin's picture, saying, with reference to the recent Crimea controversy, "Putin: Wanted for Corruption, Crimes Against Humanity & MURDER. (If seen at the G20, promptly remove him.)"

At the entrance to this year's special exhibit, a large white sign with red lettering greets me in Czech, Russian, and *finally* English: "World War I: Prolog of the XX Century" (sic). A TV shows the opening to a documentary I saw twenty years ago at a film festival in Banská Bystrica. Made in the Soviet Union, it discusses the assassination, then asks, "What were the leading lights of Europe doing?" Kaiser Wilhelm sails on his yacht while Britain's George V plays tennis. True, they weren't too distraught over events in Sarajevo, but neither were most ordinary Europeans early that summer. And there's no mention of the diplomatic back-and-forth that sought to avert war.

One pre-World-War-I satirical map is labelled in Russian as "How Germans Imagine the Future Map of Europe." It shows a Teutonic Empire stretching from England and the Netherlands all to way to Estonia. Which may be only a slight exaggeration of some of Germany's designs on eastern lands. The idea of *Lebensraum* (living space) was invented in the nineteenth century – though the Nazis brought it to a much more frightful reality. But there's a curious, inadvertent message in this pic, as it shows an independent "Kingdom of Poland." That country hadn't been allowed to exist since the 1790s, partitioned among Germany, Austria and Russia. I doubt Kaiser Wilhelm would have actually favored a reunited Poland; the tsar even less so. Of the three partitioning powers, Russia did the most to assimilate the Poles, in terms of language and religion. Austria allowed them the most freedom.

The displays are full of mannequins in period costumes and uniforms, military and civilian, as well as nurses in long dresses like the nun's habits these uniforms originated from. An awful lot of the exhibit items are on loan from Russian museums. A Putinesque reminder of long-standing Czech ties with brother Slavs from the east?

Back at the hostel I nap. Thank God things are quiet. I wake and check email, sprawled on the white couch. When the Moroccan receptionist finishes a phone conversation in Czech, I engage him in conversation. "*Jak dlouho tady bydlíte?* How long have you been living here?"

"Three years. But... wait a minute... you're American, right? How do you know Czech?"

I recount the story of my six years in Slovakia, followed by graduate studies in Slavic.

"That's good. You know, I like Czech. But, whenever I try to talk to the locals, they either switch to English, or they speak so fast—and so colloquially—I don't have a chance to understand them." His vocab is decent, but his grammar is all over the place. Czech has so many endings. Like Latin. And in this language, he's a schoolboy. Must be glad to have the practice. Since I'm not a native speaker either, it's probably less intimidating.

I get a text from violinist friend Peter with the address for his venue tonight. "No shorts or jeans," he adds. Oops. My khakis, the only proper attire other than my suit, are in my big luggage.

So I return to the station and hand the burly attendant my claim ticket. "I forgot something in my backpack. Could I just get it out real quick?"

"You have to check it out, then check it back in." He leans against a rack of suitcases and duffel bags, arms folded. "Of course, you have to pay for an extra day that way," he adds dryly.

No, he couldn't show me any sympathy.

I check it out, set it on the gray, dusty tiles, and dig through. No luck. So I start removing things. The pile on the floor grows to an embarrassing heap before I finally spot the slacks. I get out a short-sleeved blue Oxford weave for good measure, then check the pack back in.

Dressed for the evening, I stroll through Josefov, the old Jewish quarter teeming with Israeli and New York tourists, many coming to see monuments such as the grave of Rabbi Loew, the Maharal of Prague, in the Old Jewish Cemetery.

Next comes Old Town Square with the astronomical clock on its Medieval town hall. And the statue of John Huss, the fifteenth-century reformer who was burned at the stake in Constance, igniting the Hussite Wars. This was a century before Martin Luther, but Protestants look to Huss as a foreshadowing of things to come. The bronze Hus, which has regained some of its patina since its restoration seven years ago, has deep-set eyes and pointed beard. His vestments flow to the ground and into the rest of the scene: victorious Hussites from the 1400s as well as Bohemian Protestants banished in 1620 at the onset of that notoriously destructive religious conflict, the Thirty Years' War. But something is missing from the Square – a column with the Virgin Mary. It was pulled down by the 1918 equivalent of a flash mob, eager to rid themselves of reminders of the Catholic, Habsburg past.

I cross the Charles Bridge, taking in the view of the Hradčany castle complex on the far side of the Vltava. Whatever Czechs may think of Habsburg rule, Rudolf II, and later Empress Maria Theresa in the eighteenth century, carried out major expansions and renovations, which lend themselves to the current postcard view.

When I first came here in 1990, buskers and artists seemed to set up along the bridge without regulation; now everybody needs a license. At the far end of the bridge I find Russian-owned souvenir shops line the way. Twenty-some years ago, many of these folks sold *matryoshki*, the stacking dolls, from folding tables on the bridge, along with Soviet military caps, likely bought on the black market from departing Warsaw Pact soldiers.

I climb the steep streets of the Lesser Side, past embassy row, to the address Peter has given me. A few doors beyond the red, yellow, and blue flag hanging from the Romanian Legation, I find the entrance and take an elevator to the fourth floor. It's a rooftop restaurant surrounded by terra cotta tiles of neighboring buildings, echoing with conversations from thirty tables, the crunch of servers' shoes on gravel, the clang of crockery and silverware. The smooth melody lines of Peter's violin manage to pierce the noise, wafting from the far side of the dining area to my ears.

The castle complex is uphill; all but a spire of the Gothic St. Vitus' Cathedral is obscured by a thirty-foot retaining wall looming behind the restaurant. On the other side, I know from umpteen trips here, a wide pathway leads downhill from the Hradčany to the river. Tourists on that slope lean over the yellow masonry, listening to the musicians playing "Fascination."

I tell a waiter I've come to hear my friends play, in case my appearance doesn't quite fit in with this upscale crowd, mostly in business casual.

When the group finishes its set, Peter greets me with wide open arms. "Maaaark! So good to see you. How long has it been?"

"Three years. How's your son doing in conservatory?"

"Wonderful. That's why we moved here from Košice, you know."

A key development for this musical family. Peter is in white shirt and jacket, mauve tie, black slacks—all impeccably pressed—and shiny black shoes. He smiles warmly and turns his blue eyes, a rarity for Roma, as he introduces me to his bassist and guitarist, Joe and Andrei, who wear designer jeans, dress shoes, and open-collared shirts.

We shake hands and sit at a small table to the side. Andrei and Joe, like Peter, speak Slovak rather than Czech.

"I'm from Rimavská Sobota," says Andrei, who's Peter's and my age. He nods toward the younger, shyer man. "Joe's from Bratislava. We're both Hungarians." This now makes at least a half-dozen Roma from southern Slovakia that I've met who identify as Magyars.

"We just started playing together here in Prague a few months ago." Peter shifts in his white plastic chair away from the hot late-afternoon sun. "Total coincidence. This is our first gig here, by the way. I'm a bit nervous." He stands to remove his jacket.

Andrei starts talking in Hungarian to Joe. Maybe about me? Peter interrupts, addressing me in Magyar, "You haven't forgotten Hungarian, have you?"

"*Soha sincs*. Not at all." Then I wince and admit, "Actually, I don't remember it all that well."

Still, the four of us manage to exchange some basic small talk in that language.

Peter puts his jacket back on for the next set. I sip a white wine to relaxed old Viennese operetta standards, followed by the Beatles "Michelle." The diners take more notice at a bouncy version of "Mack the Knife." Soon even some of the spectators up on the retaining wall are clapping along.

As they sit back down, Andrei apologizes to Joe for his style of thumb-plucking low notes and strumming chords on the offbeat. "Of course you've got the bottom part. I'm just used to playing without a bassist. Old habit."

"Don't worry about it," says Joe. "You didn't drown me out with that little thing." We all chuckle.

A minute later Joe and Andrei switch to Romani. Is this a way of leaving me, the gadjo, out of the conversation? Well, these two don't really know me yet. Maybe it wasn't such a good idea for Peter to invite me to their first gig here.

He puts me at ease by testing the few phrases of Romani I know, an exercise we did routinely years ago. "*Ko beshavel pri lavuta?* Who's playing the violin?"

"*Peter beshavel pri lavuta,*" I respond like a schoolboy.

Everyone laughs.

Then a server asks them to play "Happy Birthday" for a group of guests. They're on a balcony with three other tables overlooking the rest of the rooftop – seems kind of exclusive. The men, almost as well-groomed as the women, wear suits – minus ties. The fifteen people converse in Dutch, French, and English. A bottle of Dom Perignon rests, tilted like the cross on St. Stephen's crown, in an ice bucket. Peter motions for me to join them. I'm surprised – but then it could be an advantage to have a native English speaker lead the singing.

A man of forty hands Peter a twenty-Euro tip as we walk away.

During this break a server brings food. To my delight, there's a fourth plate. Singing for supper with an old buddy – just what I came here for. The chicken breast in buttery lemon sauce—not a typical Czech dish—goes nicely with my second glass of crisp white.

I chat with the guys during their breaks and sing along, quietly at the table, on a few more songs. Afterwards, Peter and I stroll down the winding street named for Pavel Neruda, whose nineteenth-century "Tales of the Lesser Side," set in this neighborhood, have become mandatory reading for Czech schoolkids. When we reach a metered parking lot, Peter offers me a ride home in his Volvo station wagon. It's only two years old and immaculate. He must be doing well.

As he drops me off, he says, "Come join us tomorrow at the Three Knights. It's not as fancy a place, but you'll have fun."

* * *

On my final full day in Prague, I take a stroll down Wenceslas Square, where students protested the Soviet invasion of 1968, and where again in 1989 they assembled to call for an end to Communist Party rule: the Velvet Revolution. I turn onto "National Avenue," and near a subway entrance, my attention is grabbed by an accordion playing the dark opening notes of Bach's "Toccata and Fugue in D Minor." A short, rotund man runs his pudgy fingers up the keyboard and holds the suspended chord that resolves into a bright, lingering major before lighting into the fast phrases, which dance up and down the scale. At the finish, a crowd of thirty claps and tosses money into his azure plastic tip bucket.

He speaks Russian to a man selling the musician's CDs from a small wire rack like those found on department store counters. Approaching the accordionist in the same language, I discover he's from Crimea. Uh-oh, I think, and try to come up with a way to keep the conversation on music. Because if he's an ethnic Russian, he's probably glad Putin re-attached the peninsula to the "old homeland." The territory has relatively few ethnic Ukrainians. Gorbachev said that the annexation this past March "corrected a historical mistake." Ever since Khrushchev signed the region over to the Ukrainian SSR back in 1954, rumors have circulated that he was drunk when he did so. But Putin's use of "little green men," Russian soldiers and operatives in camouflage unmarked for nationality, while not a clear-cut violation of international law, was certainly in legally turgid waters. Since holding a referendum with no constitutional precedent defies the rule of law, the peninsula's status—Russian or Ukrainian—will remain a diplomatic fly in the ointment for years to come, as few Western countries will recognize the annexation. Even China has not done so.

To my relief, the tubby, grey-haired musician complains, "Crimea is Ukraine, not Russia. Putin stole my homeland. Now where am I to go?"

I bite my lower lip in sympathy and shake his hand. "I hope this matter resolves peacefully and you can go back."

"I'm probably going to have to stay in Kiev with relatives. But for now I'm travelling around Europe."

Europe, hm. Like the Russians on the bus to Dubrovnik, he regards Russia and Europe as separate entities. Russia is part of, and dominates the space of "Eurasia," corresponding roughly to the expanse of the thirteenth-century Mongol Empire.

"Best of luck!" I tell the accordionist, who waves back from his miniscule folding chair.

I enter the station and, descending the escalator to the platform, ponder the implications of the crisis. Putin's actions were devious, if not lawless. Not to mention clever and innovative. The use of misinformation by troll farms to cast doubt on... well, everything. Stefan Zweig, that stubbornly independent thinker, remarked in *The World of Yesterday* on how rapidly propaganda spread after the outbreak of World War I. Things haven't changed that much, it seems.

Back in March, I interviewed an older Ukrainian-America friend, Orest Pelech. He's a retired history Ph.D. living on Virginia's Eastern Shore, the rural place I grew up in – and after years of wandering the world once again call home. I was writing a newspaper story on this gentleman's "local connection" to events abroad. Orest was born in a displaced person's camp in post-war Germany – Stalin was ethnically cleansing his family's part of Ukraine at the time. That was in the western portion around L'viv – which, he emphasized, had always been under the influence of either Poles or Austrians. "My parents were not touched by the Russian language or culture," he said, until World War II. "They were fluent in both Polish and German."

L'viv had long belonged to Poland, earlier the Polish-Lithuanian Commonwealth, which at one time stretched from the Baltic Sea nearly to the Black Sea, and in the early 1600s had been poised to dominate Russia. In decline since then, Poland was infamously carved up among Russia, Prussia, and Austria in the late 1700s. In three separate waves of partitioning. "Peeled and devoured like an artichoke," was the commonly used image of dividing up first the outer parts, then the middle, and finally its core. Vanished from the map until it was reconstituted at the end of World War I.

This reality didn't reflect well on Austria, since the Polish King Jan Sobieski III had come to the rescue of Vienna when it was besieged by the Ottoman Turks in 1683. That saved Christian Europe, by many reckonings. It was the first major cooperation between the Polish-Lithuanian Commonwealth and the Holy Roman Empire, then under the rule of the Habsburg Leopold I. I can't help but see it as a precedent for an EU expanded to the east and north, as it has been in recent years.

The British writer G.K. Chesterton remarked on Austria's ingratitude at repaying the Poles in such a manner. The Austrian aristocrat, monarchist, historian, and devoted Catholic Erik Ritter von Kuehnelt-Leddihn referred to the Partitions as the geopolitical "Original Sin" of modern Europe. Indeed, its effects were deleterious from both a moral and a pragmatic standpoint: partitioning helped foster World War I by removing the buffer zone between expansionist Germany and expansionist Russia.

But this reality always makes me wonder: where does Central Europe end and Eastern Europe begin? Historically, culturally, even cities like L'viv belong to Central Europe. Czechs get tired of being called "Eastern Europeans" – their capital, after all, is farther west than Vienna. In my travels and writing, I try to emphasize that, like those western Ukrainians, the Czechs and Slovaks have never been ruled by tsars, but rather (in the past several centuries) by Austrian emperors, or else Hungarian or Polish kings. Crimea, even Odessa, may belong to Eastern Europe, but not Prague or Budapest. Long live the idea, the ideal, of Central Europe!

After riding a few stops on the metro, I wait a half-hour at a grungy station under an elevated highway. The bus takes me across a stretch of the Vltava you'll never see on postcards: nineteenth-century buildings that haven't had a fresh coat of paint in forty years, interspersed with gray socialist-era high-rises. Then we come to a neighborhood with more crumbling plaster and masonry. Potholed blacktop, rather than neatly lain cobblestones, are the norm in areas like this that don't bring in big tourist dollars. I find the Military

History Museum behind a courtyard where grass grows through cracks in the concrete.

Inside is the special exhibit *In the Trenches of World War I.* Dummies in gray Austro-Hungarian uniforms crouch behind barbed wire and log barricades. A map of 1914 Europe covers one wall. Short artillery pieces alternate with waist-high vitrines displaying rifles, medals, grenades, bayonets, and a field telephone. A foot-long shell has been "dissected"—like an illustration in an anatomy textbook—to reveal scores of lead shrapnel balls. I flinch at the thought of them tearing through twenty-year-old flesh, imagining multiple pinpoints of pain in my own torso.

After viewing the period uniforms and recruitment posters, of which I've seen plenty on this trip, I find a novel approach to the war. The museum has posted the biographies of ten Czech soldiers, showing their boyhood homes in Bohemia and Moravia, then following them through the war. One dies in 1916, another returns home lamed, another fights all the way through. Some are captured. One who surrendered to the Russians joins the Czechoslovak Legion, one of the most curious military units to come out of the conflict.

The Legion was formed when anti-Habsburg Czech and Slovak leaders in exile realized that many such prisoners of war would welcome the opportunity to fight *against* their old masters. Naturally tsarist authorities feared the newly formed units would only return to fight for Austria-Hungary, but eventually they grasped that these Slavs would rather battle for their independence from Austria-Hungary. But shortly after Russia relented came the two revolutions of 1917. (The February Revolution was the real one, since it led to Nicholas II's abdication in March, and Lenin didn't return from Swiss exile until the month after that. The October thing was more like a coup in which the Bolsheviks, by no means the only party of the Left, seized power from the Provisional Government.) The resulting civil war quickly enveloped the Legionnaires. Their basic sentiments were anti-Red, though not necessarily pro-White. They managed to take over a thousand miles of the Trans-Siberian Railway, advancing on Yekaterinburg in the Urals, where Nicholas II and his family were being held. The Bolsheviks, fearful of losing their hostages, shot all the Romanovs in the basement of the now-infamous Ipatiev House.

I stumble down the uneven street to the nearest tram stop, the death of empires on my mind. It occurs to me that, while the Russian *monarchy* came to an end, the geopolitical great power was resurrected as the Soviet Union. It contained nearly a hundred languages and nationalities. Assimilation under pressure or by force was far greater—both under the tsars and under the Communists, especially Stalin—than had ever been the case with the Habsburgs. Austria-Hungary may have been a "cage of nations," as many sarcastically called it toward the end, but Imperial Russia was far worse. A couple of Czech/Slovak pan-Slavists in the mid-nineteenth century initially adored Russia for being a country where Slavs were in command. But after visiting the tsarist behemoth, and seeing its autocracy in action, they had second thoughts. Probably their observations of the treatment of Poles following the Partitions had something to do with it. "Congress Poland," as the Russian partitioned areas were known, was subject to fierce Russification, both religious (conversion to Orthodoxy) and linguistic. Almost everyone of Polish origin I've discussed the Partitions with says that the Austrians (partly due to their Catholic religious affinity, of course) treated the Poles best of all the partitioning powers.

Still, the Czechs had suffered considerably under Austrian rule, the most bitter memory being the aftermath of 1620's Battle of the White Mountain, the first major conflict of the Thirty Years' War. Retribution was swift – Czech Protestant nobles behind the rebellion that led to the battle were executed and their heads placed on hooks at the west end of Charles Bridge. Catholics and German-speakers came to dominate the society. In all fairness, the Czechs' lot had improved during the nineteenth century: they gained full male suffrage (without property requirements) and their literacy rate had nearly caught up to that of the Germans (ninety-seven versus ninety-eight percent). But they were still lower on the social ladder. Who can blame them—or other peoples—for wanting out?

Unlike Tsar Nicholas II, at least Karl I was never executed. In November 1918 he signed a document allowing the peoples of the monarchy to determine their fate. While it wasn't an abdication, he was sent into Swiss exile four months later.

On that very day, Stefan Zweig was passing in the opposite direction, from a Switzerland untouched by war – except for all the spies in the country. He got off in Feldkirch, Austria, the border station near the Rhine. In 2000, I saw that station from my window on a rail journey from Vienna to Liechtenstein. There is little in the way of platforms, so Zweig was doubtless standing in the open railyard waiting for the next express east when Karl's train came rolling in. He writes:

> Upon alighting I became aware of an odd restlessness among the customs officers and police.... At last came the bell that announced the approach of a train from the Austrian side. The police lined up, the officials piled out

of their offices.... Slowly, almost majestically, it seemed, the train rolled near, ... a train deluxe. The locomotive stopped.... Then I recognized behind the plate glass window of the car Emperor Karl, the last Emperor of Austria standing with his black-clad wife, Empress Zita. I was startled; the last Emperor of Austria, heir of the Habsburg dynasty, which had ruled for seven hundred years, was forsaking his realm! .... The tall serious man at the window was having a last look at the hills and homes, at the people of his land.

At this moment, Zweig realized the empire of his youth was indeed no more.

* * *

In the Three Knights tavern in the evening, I meet Peter, Joe and Andrei once more. The large one-star restaurant, with sidewalk tables, several dining rooms on the ground floor and several in the basement, is hopping. My buddies move from one space to another, playing first for German, then for Czech, then Russian tourists. These have come by the busload, and are now eating, drinking, and chatting noisily at long tables. I'm left to find a tiny corner table in the cellar. I try to order roast duck with red cabbage, a succulent Bohemian specialty, but they're all out. So I get the next best thing: pork, bread dumplings, and sauerkraut.

During a break, Peter appears downstairs. "Mark, can you sing something with us? We've got a group of Russians in one room, and Brits in the next."

"Do you know 'Those Were the Days'?"

"Sure. What key?"

"F-sharp minor."

A minute later, I'm softly singing the opening, "Once upon a time there was a tavern..." and building up to the refrain. The UK crowd claps along joyfully. When things quiet down, I turn to the Russian table and sing in their language, and they join in. We go back and forth a couple of times.

"What else can you do?" asks Peter.

"'Moon River.' C major."

The English-speaking crowd joins in on this quieter tune. Peter motions for me to pass around a basket for tips. We get about two to five Euros from each patron, in various currencies. At the end of the song, Peter takes the basket to a back room and gathers the money, a bit wide-eyed at the take. Okay, so he is in it for the money, but why not? He does it for a living.

The bassist slaps me on the back. "Great job! You take your singing pretty seriously. I see you've studied technique."

"Thank you." I've finally found the "right Gypsies."

Peter drives the four of us home, with me lying in the back of the station wagon alongside the bass, which takes up part of the rear seat. I look up through the back glass as we pass by the four-story buildings. A curious view, after all the tram rides, sightseeing buses, and walking tours of Prague I've taken.

Ah, how the city reflects its Habsburg heritage: similar monuments and architecture, the linguistic cross-fertilization that enriched the empire's dozen languages, with all the culinary commonalities: Wiener schnitzel, *Apfelstrudel*, goulash, slivovitz. Austria-Hungary has bequeathed so much to today's cultures: Freud, Mozart, polka. And for many who were born well after the demise of Austria-Hungary, even for some, like me, with no ancestry in Central Europe, it will remain a kind ghost of the past, reminding us to strive for a polity of supranational tolerance. And every time we hear a Viennese waltz, or the old *Kaiserlied*, the Radetzky March, the Blue Danube Waltz, or Mozart, the grandeur of this lost world will sparkle in our memory like the hundreds of thumbnail-sized pieces of Bohemian crystal in the chandeliers in Vienna's Musikverein.

Peter drops off the other guys—and Joe's bass, freeing a space for me—and takes me to the station to get my checked bag. In front of my hostel, he puts his flashers on and stops with two wheels up on the sidewalk of the narrow, cobblestone street.

"Mark, I'm so glad we could get together."

"It's been a while since I've, uh, made music with Gypsies like this. Thanks!"

"Any time, Mark. You'll be back in Europe before long, won't you?"

"I sure hope so."

He smiles and gives me a man-hug. I wave as he drives off.

* * *

The next morning, I get up before my alarm clock goes off, gather my things and march three blocks to the metro station. I know the drill after a dozen times in Prague. Take the green line to the end, get on bus 119. Then all the way to the airport, now named for Václav Havel.

After the plane takes off, I lean back, scan the movie menu, and select *Grand Budapest Hotel*. The opening text appears: *Zubrowka, once the seat of an empire.*

I open my copy of *The World of Yesterday* to the familiar phrase at the beginning. "I was born in 1881 in a great and mighty empire, in the monarchy of the Habsburgs. But do not look for it on the map; it has been swept away without a trace."

From the map, perhaps, but not from my heart.

EPILOGUE

Eight years have passed since my journey. I've not had the chance to return to Europe, but I have travelled back in time to the old Austria-Hungary, and not just in my imaginings or in listening to operettas! I've translated materials for Americans researching their genealogy, examined a passport from the 1870s with the image of Franz Joseph I, "Emperor of Austria, Apostolic King of Hungary, King of Bohemia, etc." and birth certificates with stamps bearing his image. Those stamps were not for postage but rather had to be bought for certain documents to be recognized; their sale was a means of recovering administrative costs. They remind me how ever-present the emperor's face was in those days. Also, recalling that I had to buy similar stamps in the 1990s before I could submit visa renewal applications for Slovakia, I now know that the modern versions were a holdover from the Empire. I expect to continue learning such things for years to come.

More importantly, I've received an education in the perspective of the poor, ordinary folk from the Habsburg lands. One project was translating an Austro-Hungarian soldier's "book of days" – not a diary, but a sort of memory book, with various entries written by army buddies. A hundred twenty pages long, it covers this young Czech's years of service, mostly spent in the Trentino region of today's Italy. It contains humorous rhymes, some quite racy, among them a play on the Lord's Prayer with words like "Our military Father [Emperor Franz Joseph] who dwellest in Vienna... give us daily a double-liter of beer, so that we can sing better." It contains a ditty about his platoon drilling in the karst mountains of northern Italy – "get your butts up that hill, you bunch of wussies!" their sergeant barks. Some of the verses, written in various hands, are accompanied by lovely and colorful, if amateur, illustrations: a soldier and his girlfriend under a willow tree here, a tombstone there. Many verses speak of a deceased young lover – a reminder that life back then could easily be cut short by diseases or infections which could be treated routinely nowadays. And of course, there's always the dreaded Dear John letter. The young Czech soldier in question, serving in an Italian-speaking area, feels solidarity with the locals – and also pines away for "home," which to him means the Czech Lands more than Austria-Hungary.

I've also translated letters, fragile ones in fading ink, in eastern and western dialects of Slovak. Written by women to immigrant relatives in the U.S., they provide a feminine perspective to balance that of the military guys: the struggle to provide food for family, fears of seduction leading to unwanted pregnancy, a child lost shortly after birth. They also include scenes of economic chaos following the breakup of Austria-Hungary, and the later division of the Cold War. One correspondent lived in Sub-Carpathian Ruthenia, which belonged to Czechoslovakia between the wars but was attached to the Ukrainian SSR in 1945, part of Stalin's westward expansion. The other lived near the banks of the Morava River, just north of where it meets the Danube, very close to both Vienna and Bratislava. After several families escaped to the West, a nearby village was razed in 1953 to build Berlin-Wall-type fortifications to keep people from leaving the Czechoslovak Socialist Republic.

While such experiences round out my knowledge of that part of the world, my basic perspective hasn't changed. There were good things in Austria-Hungary, there were bad, but there was much worse to come in the wake of its destruction. I've also had the privilege of translating some materials related to a rabbi, born in Kraków in 1869, who moved to Bohemia to head a community there after completing his studies. After World War I, he became a loyal Czechoslovak citizen, taking part in civic celebrations, standing among other dignitaries in the grandstands for military parades. During the Austro-Hungarian days and during the First Republic, he taught religion in the schools – even in public schools, Protestant, Catholic and Jewish children would separate for such instruction a couple of hours per week. Then he went to Prague for a stomach operation in August 1939.

While he was convalescing, the Munich Pact handed Hitler the Sudetenland, which included the rabbi's town. He was stuck in Prague, trying to convince officials he was not German—though that was his native language, he was also proficient in Czech, Polish, Yiddish and Hebrew—and should not be "returned" to the Third Reich. He remained in Prague as the Nazis took over, and, as his trembling handwriting on one application shows, was horrified by his likely impending doom. After a period in Theresienstadt, during which he was seen debating and even joking with fellow rabbis, apparently reconciled to his fate, he perished in Treblinka.

And now, Europe's future seems more precarious than ever. A few years ago, Brexit seemed unlikely at best. After sixteen years as German chancellor, Angela Merkel has finally stepped down. While her policies and legacy will be debated for years, she has at least served as a bastion of stability and decency in European politics – in often-trying times. Who knows if central Europe will have such a leader again any time soon? It seems like a scaled-down version of Franz Joseph's or Queen Victoria's long reign has drawn to an end, as, indeed, has Elizabeth II's.

But of course, political arrangements we take for granted are rarely as permanent as we think. Alliances shift, just as they did before WWI. Empires fall, as they did in its aftermath. Who would have thought, before Trump, that an American president would question the purpose of NATO and cozy up to a Russian leader? And who would have thought that Putin would undertake a full-scale invasion of Ukraine? (Or that Russia's fetishism with the Latin letter Z, from tanks and personnel carriers invading Ukraine, to billboards in Moscow, would become such an unintended but grotesque parody on the totalitarian Z's in Wes Anderson's Grand Budapest Hotel?)

As a global community, we talk a lot about the "lessons of Munich," about Neville Chamberlain's foolhardy belief that accommodating Hitler on the question of ethnic Germans in Czechoslovakia would lead to "peace in our time." We also need to learn from the First World War, when a conflict between two countries, Austria and Serbia, quickly consumed Europe – and much else of the globe.

We need to learn that diplomacy must be realistic. We usually pay a high price for appeasement later on. But we also need to recognize the legitimate security concerns of the "other side."

And in order to do that, we must overcome our own biases. That means listening to the other side, which has legitimate interests – and also its own biases and phobias. To that end, I have volunteered for the website Watching America, which provides translations of opinion columns from around the world unavailable anywhere else in English. I find it disturbing to read false claims such as the idea that Ukraine is massacring ethnic Russians in Donbass with help from the CIA. But there are times when I have to challenge my own thinking and realize there are unpleasant actions that get little press in the U.S., such as documented CIA support for the Kosovar Liberation Army in the late 1990s, even as at least one Clinton administration official, special envoy to the Balkans Robert Gelbard, described the KLA as a terrorist organization – an extreme example of uncoordinated policy. These events followed closely on the heels of the 1997 admission of Czechia, Hungary and Poland to NATO.

And then came Putin as Russian premier in 1999. The U.S. invasion of Iraq in 2003 clearly signaled to him that America would not be restrained by international norms. To make matters worse the Bush administration recognized Kosovo independence in 2008, a smack in the face to the Serbs. And later that year came the "Open Door" policy for Ukraine, Georgia and others to join NATO. And then the Obama administration intervened in Libya to hasten the overthrow of Khadafi in 2011. All these events have contributed to the problem we now face in Eastern Europe.

None of this justifies Putin's actions. He is a ruthless, KGB-trained authoritarian who levelled the city of Grozny in Chechnya with total disregard for civilian death and suffering, all to get rid of supposed "terrorists." He appears willing to do the same in Ukraine to eliminate "neo-Nazis." His crackdowns on dissent in Russia, and his near-total control over information there, have led me to do volunteer translation for the UK-based site Rights in Russia. The West, perhaps even well after he leaves power, will have to take into account his paranoid view of the world, as it unfortunately is shared by many other Russians.

Stefan Zweig, as I recall in this book, expressed dismay that artists all over Europe began self-censoring and demonizing the other side. For instance, Shakespeare was banned from the stage in countries of the Central Powers, while Goethe was abhorred in Paris and London. In our times, all Russian-backed submissions to the Emmys were disqualified for 2022. There may be legitimate concerns over funding a dictator's war by buying imports from his country, but some people have reacted hysterically, removing from their bar shelves the well-known Stoli vodka, which is actually now owned by a Belgian company and produced in Latvia. Let's hope no one starts burning tomes of Pushkin and Tolstoy! The Cardiff Philharmonic orchestra has cut some Tchaikovsky works – the "1812 Overture" contains cannon fire; the title of his Symphony no. 2 ("Little Russian") is offensive to Ukrainians. And while these examples of cancelling Russian culture continue, at least at this writing, they're still playing Tchaikovsky and Borodin on classical radio.

It's worth noting, in these times of battles over historical memory, that the Marian column on Prague's Old Town Square has been reconstructed and was resurrected on its historical spot in August 2020. Similarly, a statue of the eighteenth-century Empress Maria-Theresa in Bratislava—where she was crowned as Queen of Hungary—was torn down in 1921 by Czechoslovak Legionnaires, an angry reaction to Charles I's second attempt at reclaiming the Hungarian throne. A reduced-size bronze replica was erected on the city's main square in 2018 but removed to a more obscure location shortly thereafter.

It is also refreshing to know that Slovakia made progress in encouraging Roma to participate in the 2021 census – although the use of both Romani and Hungarian languages have decreased.

* * *

Though my own future is somewhat unclear, a lot of what I've learned from the old Austria-Hungary seems part of it. Now a church organist and choir leader, I've discovered the subtleties of Schubert's "Ave Maria," a quintessentially Viennese work. I've watched my friends in the Cecilia choir performing in the cathedral for Pentecost on Slovak TV, and I know that their contributions to the culture of Košice will continue for years—maybe even generations—to come. My friend Peter's son has completed studies at the Prague Conservatory, while his daughter got an M.A. from Charles University and now sings with the family.

And so, with these thoughts of artistic achievement in mind, I'd like to turn once more from the world of politics and military matters to the arena of the arts – the side of the old Austro-Hungarian Empire that I most deeply admire: Let's join the "intellectual brotherhood" and internationalism of Stefan Zweig, Romain Rolland, and Archbishop Strossmayer. The arts speak a "higher language" than politics and guns and bombs, and music excels as an instrument of diplomacy and mutual understanding.

Though COVID put a damper on celebrations of Beethoven's two hundred fiftieth birthday in 2020, the musical world has come through with online tributes to his genius. The Beethovenhaus in Bonn collaborated with the Austrian Radio Symphony Orchestra and a thousand on-screen singers to produce a "Global Ode to Joy" video. Perhaps the greatest visionary of universal brotherhood through Beethoven has been conductor Daniel Barenboim, who holds citizenship from Israel, Palestine and Spain, in addition to his native Argentina. His project, the West-Eastern Divan Orchestra, which brings together young Arab and Jewish musicians, has performed some of my favorite renditions of Beethoven's Ninth Symphony. That glorious paean to humanity – which, we should remember, premiered in Vienna, the capital of Western classical music.

On that note, I think I'll sit back and listen to their "Ode to Joy" from the final movement, the "Anthem of Europe" that drew tears from my eyes in Sarajevo. And I'll raise a glass of white wine spritzer, that old Austro-Hungarian favorite, to a better future for Europe and the world.

ACKNOWLEDGEMENTS

I'd like to thank all who have made an impact in various ways while I wrote this book. My mentors Lenore Hart and David Poyer helped immensely with several rounds of chapter drafts in their Writers' Workshop at Eastern Shore's Own Arts Center in Belle Haven, Virginia. Lenore helped me shape the work further outside the Workshop and encouraged me to enter Hidden River Arts' Panther Creek Nonfiction contest. Among my fellow students in the Writer's Workshop who listened to and critiqued several chapters were: David McCaleb, Joan LeBlanc, Ken Sutton, Kenny Walker and Frances Williams. Debra Leigh Scott of Hidden River Arts made countless invaluable suggestions as the manuscript was being honed into its present form, helping me to craft a continuity of theme and tone that I could not have achieved on my own.

My high school history teacher, John Peccia, first provoked my curiosity about Austria-Hungary and the assassination in Sarajevo. He and others encouraged me by following my journey on Facebook. Finally, there are those friends, whom I include among "Ferdinand and Friends," who made my trip more enjoyable—or at least less painful at times—and improved my historical and cultural itinerary.

To name just a few: Marian Kuštán, Peter Balogh, Alena Belohorská Molnárová, "Fero" and the *Martinský spevokol* chorus in Martin, Slovakia, Vilo and the St. Cecilia choir of Košice, Slovakia, Neno from Sarajevo, and Mirjana of the hostel in Split, Croatia. A final shout-out goes to my parents, who were very understanding and encouraging when I was busy preparing the manuscript.

CPSIA information can be obtained
at www.ICGtesting.com
Printed in the USA
LVHW042115140523
746971LV00004B/371